A PSYCHOLOGY OF THE SOUL

FROM THE INFINITE INTO THE FINITE

Herbert Bruce Puryear, PhD

Herbert Puryear – A Psychology of the Soul

Second Edition

New Paradigm Press

ISBN: 978-0-9634964-1-6

Printed in the U.S.A.

Herbert Puryear – A Psychology of the Soul

Dedicated with great appreciation for the guidance and inspiration of my three muses

Anne Puryear, Edgar Cayce
and Bill Roberts

Preface

This second edition clarifies several vital passages for easier readability and study. Furthermore, there are image embellishments and additions. The Lyden-Pineal connection is clarified and the importance of the Cayce *Secret of the Golden Flower* parallels is stressed.

I do not consider myself a scholar, an intellectual, or an academic. Rather, I see myself as a student and a seeker. As such, when I discover something that excites me, I feel compelled to share it with anyone who might be interested. In that sense, I also think of myself as a teacher. This study on the nature of the soul is not intended to be comprehensive—indeed, such an ambition would be impossible given the vastness of the subject. Accordingly, I have titled this work *A* Psychology of the Soul rather than *The* Psychology of the Soul.

My goal has been to explore this topic as deeply as I am able. I take inspiration from historical journeys into the unknown, such as the Lewis and Clark expedition into the American Northwest and John Wesley Powell's daring exploration of the Colorado River. These stories of bold inquiry encourage me in my own intellectual and spiritual exploration.

The ideas I present here are not entirely new, but they are shaped by a lifetime of personal interest and experience. My hope is that this work might chart a course for future explorers, or at the very least, inspire others to engage in their own deeper studies. In my view, there is nothing more important—to individuals, to schools, to churches, and to charitable institutions—than gaining a clearer understanding of who we are and why we are here. Some people possess straight-line, linear minds; I tend to think in associations and analogies, and that inclination is reflected throughout my writing.

I approach this work with the mind of a scientist, shaped by both interest and formal training. If some of these pages seem too philosophical or metaphysical, let me clarify my scientific intentions. In the text, I discuss the two essential steps in scientific advancement: experimental research and the development of theories that adequately explain the findings. This book represents an effort to construct a theoretical framework that corresponds to existing research. Parapsychologists have amassed considerable empirical data, but they have yet to develop a psychological or physiological theory that is truly adequate to explain their findings. Some of my graduate school peers once argued that Einstein was not a true scientist because he conducted no experimental research. Yet his contributions to science are indisputable.

For scriptural references, I rely primarily on the King James Version (KJV) of the Bible, for a variety of reasons. Although some are put off by its archaic language, I view it as a classic work of art—akin to the masterpieces of Michelangelo, Mozart, or Rembrandt. I also consult other translations for comparison, especially when seeking clarity on particular verses. However, one must consider the translators' intentions. Some modern versions, aimed solely at readability, lose the deeper meaning of certain passages. Others are heavily shaped by contemporary theological views. In contrast, I believe the KJV translators were more attuned to the original authors' intent and preserved more of the symbolic depth in their work.

The challenge with reading the Bible often lies in the reader's expectations—particularly whether one chooses to believe in it or not. Some people have rejected the Bible entirely, sometimes due to offense taken at a single verse or two, often from Paul's writings. I view the biblical authors as psychics—some more gifted or attuned than others. The central question is not whether the text is divinely inspired, but whether you allow yourself to be inspired by it in your own response. Like a great poem, a single phrase may stir your soul and lift your spirit. Jesus warned the religious leaders of His time: "Thus have ye made the commandment of God of none effect by your tradition." (Matthew 15:6). For an enriching alternative perspective, consider George Lamsa's translation of the Peshitta from the original Aramaic—the language Jesus spoke. Aramaic is richly idiomatic, and any student of languages knows the challenges of literal translation, especially with idioms. Despite these complexities, the Bible remains one of the most influential and important books in human history.

Portions of this book are greatly enriched by the contribution of Bill Roberts, an advanced student of the research of Robert

Monroe and William Tiller. Roberts shares an in-depth understanding of the essential insights arising from the remarkable work of these two great pioneers. These themes are touched upon and affirmed by the Cayce Readings.

Repetition in this text is intentional because the same ideas or concepts may be relevant to and appropriately emphasized in different contexts.

The ideas in this book may prove deeply challenging—perhaps even heretical—to both scientific and Christian communities. For that reason, Part I outlines my personal journey, providing context for how I arrived at these insights and supporting the notion that I am, in some measure, qualified to engage with such a profound topic.

Acknowledgments

I AM DEEPLY and continuingly grateful for the opportunities in my life that have brought to me a greater understanding of the meaning and purposes of our lives in human bodies on the planet earth. This book, especially, is the outcome of all of my life; and so, I am appreciative of so very many - of my parents, teachers, pastors, friends and supporters. The most important books in my life have been given to me by my friends, so if there is a book that has meant something special to you, give a copy to a friend. If this book becomes meaningful to you, pass it along.

I am grateful for the excellent work of Matt Davis and David Stipes for the cover art and figures and for the unending help of Bill Roberts.

I am most appreciative of the love and support of my beloved wife, Anne, author of Stephen Lives, and psychic channel comparable to the channel, Edgar Cayce. These two, along with the Bible have been the richest sources of my studies and inspiration. I am grateful!

CONTENTS

Preface v

Acknowledgments ix

PART 1 - From the Infinite to the Finite 1

Summary 37

PART 2 – A Psychology of the Soul 43

Chapter 1 – Foundations of Our Thinking 45

Monotheism 49

The Scientific World View 51

Monism 52

The Soul 58

Personhood 59

Continuity and Karma 62

Our Search for The Truth 63

Science as A Biped 65

Science and The Bible 68

Lawfulness 72

The Lord's Prayer and the Seven Centers 74

Chapter 2 – Psychics, Parapsychology and Psychical Research 79

The Edgar Cayce Story 79

The Good Shepherd 83

Psychics 84
Parapsychology 88
Scientists with Half-Closed Minds 92
Psychical Research 95
Chapter 3 – Models and Theories 99
Chapter 4 – States of Consciousness 113
Experiencing Elevated Consciousness 117
Chapter 5 – The Archetypal Bible 123
Archetypal Mantras 131
Morphic Resonance 132
Chapter 6 – Jesus, the Way 141
Spiritual History 143
The Psychology of Life 146
Chapter 7 – A Search For God 159
Mantras 162
Chapter 8 – The Revelation 165
The Silver Cord 189
The Marriage in Heaven 191
Chapter 9 – Ontogeny and the Origin of Evil 193
Chapter 10 – The Secret of the Golden Flower 203
Chapter 11 – Religions and Archetypes 221
Hinduism 221

Understanding the Anti-Christ 224
More on Hinduism..228
Archetypes and Biochemistry..229
The Tibetan Dorje..231
The Wizard of Oz and Temptation 234
Chapter 12 - Destiny...239

PART 1

FROM THE INFINITE INTO THE FINITE

THE CENTRAL CHALLENGE of all religions has been to understand the relationship between God and humankind. Terminology can complicate this inquiry—whether we refer to the Infinite as the Universe, the Divine, the One, God, Om, Yahweh, Allah, or even the Void. Still, the essential question remains: is a relationship between the Infinite and an individual human being possible—and if so, what is the nature of that relationship? This is the very question posed by the Psalmist: "What is man, that thou art mindful of him?" (Ps. 8:4)

My own search for an answer to this question has led me to the thesis that *a person may be defined as the process and record of the expression of the Infinite into the Finite*! So, I want to share some of the origins of these thoughts which I recall as having been specifically significant for me in the development of my understanding of this theory.

From an early age, I was deeply interested in both science and religion. As a child, I eagerly read the science articles in my father's *Popular Mechanics* magazines, and I still recall the sense of wonder I felt during my first Vacation Bible School. I must have been an unusual kid—I actually looked forward to Sunday School. I was captivated by the stories of biblical characters, and especially intrigued by the figure of Jesus. The music also moved me: *"I've got the peace that passeth understanding down in my heart"* and *"Jesus loves the little children, red and yellow, black and white..."* I grew up with a continuing curiosity and reverence for these things.

My first mystical experience was one that many people share: an awe-inspiring awareness of the night sky. One evening in 1938, I tagged along as my older brother played tennis at the town park. As we walked home through the quiet, moonless night, I suddenly noticed the sky. In a small town of 4,000 people, at an elevation of 3,500 feet, there was no light or atmospheric pollution—just the brilliant sweep of stars, including the radiant band of the Milky Way. Even now, the memory of that moment still stirs me. The sheer majesty of it seemed to point directly to eternity and infinity.

One night our church held a revival. The evangelist was a retired railroad engineer named Brother Pons. He was filled with dramatic stories about the people he had served. I was moved to go down at the altar call. I became a declared believer, was baptized, and my faith grew deeper.

This was not without problems. Around the age of ten or twelve, every kid begins to ask questions—especially about the troubling theology that nonbelievers are sent to an eternal hell forever and ever. At that age, we are old enough to recognize the issue but still too young to have been thoroughly indoctrinated into accepting such a cruel teaching. What an ugly picture this belief paints of a God of love and forgiveness! I didn't get my questions answered, so I settled for some intuitive sense that there were, in truth, better answers.

After the outbreak of World War II, we moved from Wellington to Lubbock. At the First Baptist Church in Lubbock, I was introduced to new perspectives. The church had a larger group of young people, a highly educated ministry, and a wonderful choir with beautiful instrumental music. I continued my search.

One Sunday, something changed. I left church with a profound conviction that the Bible was calling me to more than weekly attendance. If I was to continue in this faith, I would need to go deeper. I bought a large-print Bible from a discount drugstore and began studying. The more I read, the more engaged and convinced I became: *this book had to be taken seriously!*

In high school, my best friend and I came across a book that proved to be both literally and meaningfully life-changing. It marked the true beginning of my special interest in the idea that we are a *Finite expression of the Infinite*. The book was titled *I Dare You*.

This book played an important role in orienting me toward a well-balanced life. The author emphasized the importance of developing the physical, mental, spiritual, and social aspects of our being. But what stood out most for me was a legend he included—one that so captivated me it became almost a personal meditation. Over the past several decades, I've retold it scores, maybe hundreds of times. Here is the legend, as related by W.H. Danforth in *I Dare You*:

> At one time all men on earth were gods, but men so sinned and abused the Divine that Brahma, the god of all gods, decided that the godhead should be taken away from man and hid some place where he would never again find it to abuse it.
>
> "We will bury it deep in the earth," said the other gods.

"No, said Brahma, "because man will dig down in the earth and find it."

"Then we will sink it in the deepest ocean," they said.

"No," said Brahma, "because man will learn to dive and find it there, too."

"We will hide it on the highest mountain," they said.

"No," said Brahma, 'because man will someday climb every mountain on the earth and again capture the godhead."

"Then we do not know where to hide it where he cannot find it," said the lesser gods.

"I will tell you," said Brahma, "hide it down in man himself. He will never think to look there."

And that is what they did. Hidden down in every man is some of the divine.

Ever since then he has gone over the earth digging, diving and climbing, looking for that god quality which all the time is hidden down within himself.

This legend reminded me not only of the Biblical story of the fall of man and the story of the Prodigal Son, but also gave me a new clue as to why human beings seem so disconnected in consciousness from their awareness of the divine. I had already noticed that Psalm 82 declared, *"You are gods, children of the Most High, all of you,"* and I was familiar with Psalm 8.

In 1946, the long-anticipated Revised Standard Version (RSV) of the Bible was released, and it introduced a surprising change to Psalm 8. In the King James Version (KJV), the verse reads: *"What is man that thou art mindful of him? For thou hast made him a little lower than the angels."* The RSV translated this instead as, *"Thou hast made him little less than God."* Fascinatingly, the New Revised Standard Version (NRSV) later revised this again—this time to *"a little lower than God."* It was as if the editors recognized the powerful implication of the verse, affirmed it for a moment, and then retreated. *"Ye are gods."*

As part of its broader educational programming, Lubbock High School once hosted a stage hypnotist named Franz Polgar. He was truly extraordinary. I saw him perform three times over a three-year period. Later, I found his autobiography, *The Story of a Hypnotist.* He had been injured in World War I, and upon awakening in the hospital, discovered that he had become clairvoyant. Other cases like this exist—Peter Hurkos is another example of someone who became psychic after a serious injury. These cases suggest that *there is a physical component to psychic abilities*. After seeing Polgar, I tried to learn everything I could about hypnosis.

At the same time, I kept reading and re-reading the New Testament. I still felt that I needed to decide whether I was going to take the story seriously—or set it aside. If I chose to take it seriously, I had to confront the fact that many of its most central teachings—such as Jesus's promises about prayer, the coming of the Holy Spirit, and even the virgin birth—were either not being taught or were viewed with skepticism, even by those proclaiming the Bible most loudly.

As much as I loved the old, old story, there seemed to be a living and dynamic reality that was neither being experienced nor discussed. I knew there was more—much more—to learn and experience.

At that time, I was also reading Kipling. In *The Explorer*, he writes:

> Something hidden. Go and find it. Go and look behind the ranges —
>
> Something lost behind the Ranges. Lost and waiting for you. Go!

And the Hindu legend echoed that same call: it is hidden *"down in man himself. He will never think to look there."*

The next intimations of this theme of the godhead within us were some passages from Kahlil Gibran's *The Prophet*.

> And a man said, Speak to us of Self-Knowledge. And he answered, saying:
>
> Your hearts know in silence the secrets of the days and the nights.
>
> But your ears thirst for the sound of your heart's knowledge. You would know in words that which you have always known in thought. Then said a teacher, Speak to us of Teaching. And he said: No man can reveal to you aught but

> that which already lies half asleep in the dawning of your knowledge.
>
> The teacher who walks in the shadow of the temple, among his followers, gives not of his wisdom but rather of his faith and his lovingness. If he is indeed wise, he does not bid you enter the house of his wisdom, but rather leads you to the threshold of your own mind.

My years at Lubbock High were, overall, a very positive experience. One particularly memorable course was taught by a history teacher, Miss Scarlet. She offered a course on the Bible—as history. Imagine that being done in a public school! Protestant, Catholic, and Jewish students alike took and enjoyed the class. As probably the most influential book in the world, it should be offered in *every* school.

I also took a speech class that included some basic debating. I was a Baptist but believed that baptism was not essential for salvation, while my friend, a member of the Church of Christ, held the opposite view—that one *must* be baptized to be saved. A fellow student invited the two of us, along with several others, to her home for a friendly debate on the issue. What I discovered that night was the futility of debating as a method for uncovering truth.

During my senior year, a friend and I set out on what might best be called a vision quest. He too was interested in understanding the Bible in deeply personal and practical terms. An older friend of ours, who was preparing for the ministry, had once told us that he prayed over even the most trivial details of his day. My friend and I thought this was amusing, so we decided—half-jokingly—to try it on a weekend camping trip. We agreed that, for the duration of the trip, we would pray together and seek guidance in a spirit of openness for every action we took. When it came time to choose a campsite, we prayed and moved in the direction we felt led. We found exactly the right place. When it was time to gather firewood, we did the same—and again found what we needed. We kept this up the entire weekend.

That night, as I lay under the vast Texas sky with the coyotes howling in the distance, I had a dream. I heard a voice—clear and unmistakable—saying, *"Teach the Bible."* I experienced it as a calling. I knew it was the voice of God. It was to become my life's work.

We had felt guided throughout the weekend, even in the most mundane of activities. It seemed to me that the Infinite was expressing itself in the Finite—not only in the intricate beauty of nature surrounding us, but in the smallest choices of our own lives.

Still, the full significance of our weekend experiment didn't become clear until later, when our pre-ministerial friend gave a talk at a small country church in Shallowater. His title was *"Boys, Beans and the Bible."* He recounted our camping experience to illustrate how God is always with us, and how, when we approach life in a prayerful spirit, we can receive guidance from within on even the simplest matters.

That evening, after the service, a small group of us gathered in a side room of the church for quiet reflection and prayer. In the stillness, a brilliant light filled the room, and I felt a great hand come to rest on my shoulder. It was powerful yet gentle, burning yet healing—completely reassuring. In that moment, I knew that *He was there with me*. And I knew exactly what the prophets of old meant when they said, *"the hand of the Lord was upon me."*

Within a matter of days, I had experienced both an inner calling and a profound outer confirmation of the divine presence. During the camping trip, I had heard God from within. In the quiet of that church, I encountered God as a presence beyond myself. And yet—I knew both were the same Reality.

During high school, my mother worked in a department store. After school, I often stopped in to see her. Right next to her department was a small bookstore, and while she helped customers, I would browse the shelves. One book caught my attention: *A General Introduction to Psychoanalysis* by Sigmund Freud. At that time, in the mid-1940s, psychoanalysis was the talk of the day. I read the book with great interest—especially the chapters on dream interpretation, which comprised about half of the book. That discovery ignited what would become a lifelong fascination with dreams. I went back to the store, again and again, to find more books on psychoanalysis.

Still in high school, I was accepted into a naval aviation college program and enrolled at the University of Texas. But after those spiritual experiences—after hearing my calling—I transferred to Baylor University, planning a double major in psychology and the Bible.

In the summer of 1947, shortly after graduating high school, I read a *Reader's Digest* review of J.B. Rhine's book *The Reach of the Mind.* I immediately found and read the full book. It deeply inspired me. I felt that Rhine's research in parapsychology offered scientific support for many of the events described in the Bible—events that had long been dismissed as mere belief.

When I got to Baylor, I tried to share my excitement about this research. The science professors were offended. The Bible professors were scandalized. Their negative reactions only strengthened my conviction that parapsychology was important—and that it deserved serious attention.

In my English composition class, my first term paper was titled *"Psychoanalysis and Religion."* My instructor was delighted. She said my essay stood out—quite different from the usual submissions she received from other students, many of whom were ministerial students.

Baylor was on the quarter system. My second English composition instructor, a friend of the first, was also impressed with my work. The two of them approached Professor A.J. Armstrong, then considered the world's leading expert on the English poet Robert Browning. They wanted me to have the rare opportunity of attending his senior-level class. They feared that Armstrong might not be teaching by the time I reached my senior year. With their help, I became the first freshman ever allowed to monitor the course.

One of Browning's classically beautiful and instructive poems is *Paracelsus*. Browning has Paracelsus, a seeker for the truth, saying:

> Truth is within our-selves; it takes no rise
> From outward things, whate'er you may believe.
> There is an inmost centre in us all,
> Where truth abides in fulness; and around,
> Wall upon wall, the gross flesh hems it in,
> This perfect, clear perception - which is truth
> A baffling and perverting carnal mesh
> Binds it, and makes all error: and, to know,
> Rather consists in opening out a way
> Whence the imprisoned splendour may escape,
> Than in effecting entry for a light
> Supposed to be without.

The *imprisoned splendour*, within ourselves yet bound by a baffling and perverting carnal mesh!

I saw a relationship between the Hindu legend and this passage from Deut. 30:11-14:

> For this commandment which I command thee this day, it is not hidden from thee, neither is it far off. It is not in heaven, that thou shouldst say, who shall go up for us to heaven, and bring it unto us, that we may hear it and do it? Neither is it

> beyond the sea, that thou shouldst say, who shall go over the sea for us and bring it unto us, that we may hear it, and do it? But the word is very nigh unto thee, in thy mouth, and in thy heart, that thou mayest do it.

This theme of divine truth dwelling within began to show up everywhere. I found it again in the words of the prophet Jeremiah:

> But this shall be the covenant that I will make with the house of Israel; After those days, saith the Lord, I will put my law in their inward parts, and write it in their hearts: and will be their God, and they shall be my people. And they shall teach no more every man his neighbor, and every man his brother, saying, Know the Lord: for they shall all know me. (Jer. 3: 33-34)

The writer of Hebrews echoed this same promise:

> Whereof the Holy Ghost also is a witness to us: for after that he had said before, This is the covenant that I will make with them after those days, saith the Lord, I will put my laws into their hearts, and in their minds will I write them. (Heb. 10:15-16)

Then I found this theme again—quoted, paraphrased, and interpreted in a most profound and compelling way—in Paul's letter to the Romans:

> For Christ is the end of the law for righteousness to everyone that believeth. For Moses describeth the righteousness which

> is of the law, That the man which doeth those things shall live by them. But the righteousness which is of faith speaketh on this wise, Say not in thine heart, Who shall ascend into heaven? (that is, to bring Christ down from above:) Or, Who shall descend into the deep? (that is, to bring up Christ again from the dead.) But what saith it? The word is nigh thee, even in thy mouth, and in thy heart: that is, the word of faith, which we preach. (Rom. 10:4–8)

For Paul, the author of Romans 10, the law referenced in Deuteronomy 30—written in our mouths and in our hearts—is *the Christ which is within us*. For Paul, the Law that once resided in the Ark of the Covenant—the sacred object placed in the Holy of Holies where the high priest was to meet God face to face—that Law, the Torah, had now become *the Christ*.

And for both Paul and Jesus, the body is the new temple. We are to meet Him *within ourselves*. The Law, as fulfilled by Jesus in becoming the Christ, is the Law of Love. It is the pattern of the divine within each of us, waiting to be re-discovered, awakened, and lived out in fullness. He prepared it for us from the beginning and demonstrated through His life *the Way*.

We were scheduled to meet with Professor Armstrong to discuss our plans for our term papers. I proposed writing on the theme of Browning's *imprisoned splendour* passage, integrating insights from the Hindu legend, Gibran's *The Prophet*, relevant biblical texts, and the parapsychology research I was so excited about.

I presented my idea to Dr. Armstrong. His jaw literally dropped. I have never seen such a dark, stunned expression on anyone's face. After a pause, he said quietly, *"No, I don't think that is a suitable subject."* At the time, I had no idea how seriously heretical the *godhead within* concept was in mainstream Christian theology.

Simultaneously, in the wake of my white light experience, I had begun searching for books about the Holy Spirit. I wanted to understand: What did it really mean to be *born again*—or to be *born of the Spirit*? How did such experiences happen? How could one prepare for them? To my surprise, I learned it was not considered wise to mention these questions around the Baylor Bible faculty. They were, it seemed, actively opposed to literature about the experiential side of the Holy Spirit.

Eventually, I discovered a small group of students who were quietly exploring these very topics. They circulated certain theological writings underground—especially the work of Charles Finney, one of the subjects whose white light experiences are recounted in Bucke's *Cosmic Consciousness*.

I studied Finney's *Revival Lectures* and devoured every book I could find about the baptism of the Spirit. Later, I came upon Marcus Bach's *The Inner Ecstasy*—a deeply compelling account of his own experience of baptism in the Spirit.

The encounter with Professor Armstrong, combined with what I was beginning to learn about the attitudes of the Bible professors, marked the beginning of my realization: there is deep resistance—culturally, intellectually, even emotionally—against the idea that the divine might reside within us. Over time, I came to see that this might be *humanity's most deeply resisted insight*.

Still, I pressed on. I continued reading the Bible and psychology texts. I added the literature of psychical research to my growing library. Many people in these fields insisted on their differences—psychology, religion, parapsychology, mysticism. But the Hindu legend helped me imagine something deeper: a fundamental *Oneness* beneath all these approaches. I was often reminded of the old parable about the five blind men of Hindustan—each feeling a different part of the elephant and coming away with a completely different description of what the elephant *was*.

Of all the programs at Baylor, one stood out as a bright spot. It was called "Missions." On Friday nights, we gathered in small groups and visited local churches, Black congregations, and retirement homes. We told Bible stories, sang songs, and prayed with the children and adults we met. Later, we would return to the student union to share our experiences and sing choruses in what we called "singspiration." To this day, many of those joyful, faith-filled songs still live in my memory.

One mission took us to Waco's skid row on Saturday mornings for street preaching. I gave a short sermon there. Afterward, a man in his mid-thirties approached me. He asked if I would come to his room and pray for him. He was caught in alcoholism and had reached a point of near hopelessness. I went—but as I prayed with him, I felt an unmistakable emptiness, a powerlessness. Spiritually, I knew I could not truly help him—not yet. I still had much to seek and learn. I yearned for a deeper encounter with the Holy Spirit and the kind of empowerment that would allow me to truly be of service.

In time, I grew disillusioned with my Baylor experience. I had looked forward to their Bible courses with great anticipation, but I found them lacking. In truth, the Bible course I had taken in high school had been superior. I wasn't doing well otherwise, either.

At the end of my sophomore year's second quarter, I dropped out. I had been reading Richard Halliburton's travel books, full of daring global adventures, and watching films like *Lost Horizon* and *The Razor's Edge*. Inspired by these stories, I hitchhiked to San Francisco, hoping to get a job on a freighter and make my way to Tibet. Thankfully, I lacked the stamina—and probably the luck—to pull it off. I returned to Lubbock, worked odd jobs, and wandered through a fruitless year.

Then the Korean War broke out, and I was close to being drafted. The Navy guaranteed me a spot in electronics school, so I enlisted. I brought only two books to boot camp: the Bible and *Science is a Sacred Cow*. With plenty of free time during training, I devoured everything I could find about parapsychology. Inevitably, this led me to the story of Edgar Cayce.

When I read *There Is a River* by Thomas Sugrue, I was completely prepared—intellectually, emotionally, and spiritually—for the extraordinary insights contained in the life of Edgar Cayce. That book changed the course of my life.

In *There Is a River*, I found the story of a man who had actually lived the kind of life I had only imagined. Cayce had spent his life manifesting—in thought and action—the harmony of *the God without* and *the godhead within*. Guided by a principle of Oneness, he expressed the flow of energy and insight from the divine source into human service. His only motivation was to help others. And in doing so, he became a living demonstration of what it means for the Infinite to enter the Finite.

Motivated solely by the desire to be of help to others, Edgar Cayce gave expression to the flow of energy and information from the divine without, through the divine within.

For over forty years—until shortly before his death in 1945—Edgar Cayce engaged in a practice commonly referred to as "giving Readings." These numbered over 14,000. What exactly is an Edgar Cayce Reading?

The answer depends, in part, on the degree to which one is willing to believe that the Infinite can express itself through the Finite. At the very least, that appears to be what happened in his daily work. Cayce would lie down, close his eyes, and shift his consciousness to a level where he could access all kinds of information. He would respond to questions intended to help others, drawing answers from what the Readings called the *Universal Consciousness*—or, synonymously, *God.*

Though I still had many years of undergraduate, graduate, and postdoctoral study ahead of me, the Cayce Readings quickly became—and have remained—the true foundation of my education and the wellspring of my insights. These Readings rekindled and deepened my interest in the Bible. Their approach was more profound, more coherent, more practical, and more universal than anything I had previously encountered. The Readings also revitalized my commitment to prayer and to the study of dreams. They affirmed the immeasurable value of these two inward paths to the divine. Through this work, I came to realize that I truly could follow my calling and *teach the Bible.*

I had already considered Deuteronomy 30 as a biblical parallel to the Hindu legend. But now, that chapter of the Bible took on new vitality for me. The Cayce Readings repeatedly emphasized its importance and demonstrated its relevance to a wide range of individuals, in all sorts of circumstances, and with a variety of personal needs.

I had applied for and was accepted into flight school. After many months of flight training, I completed the program and was assigned to a base just seventy miles from Virginia Beach, Virginia—headquarters of the Cayce work. On my very first weekend there, I drove up to the Beach to find the Cayces. I located the old Cayce home, and on that Sunday afternoon, I was fortunate enough to be invited into a study group already in progress. That evening, I shared a Chinese dinner with Hugh Lynn Cayce, Edgar Cayce's son.

A few months later, I received a temporary duty assignment in the area and was able to stay at the Cayce home for three weeks. During that time, I met and spoke with several people who had received readings directly from Mr. Cayce and had known him personally.

Shortly thereafter I was assigned to a tour of duty in Japan, I brought with me a stack of Cayce Readings, including an early interpretation of the Book of Revelation. I studied these materials intensely, memorizing large portions, and spent many hours in the base library exploring everything I could about psychical research.

At the time, there was a military magazine published monthly for service personnel stationed in Japan. One issue featured an article about a sixteen-year-old girl who channeled an old man with a beard. Curious, I set out to find her and receive what would be my first psychic reading. I hadn't even considered the need for an interpreter—but, by the grace of God, a former Japanese military officer fluent in English happened to be there. He had once been stationed in Mongolia, where he discovered a vast metaphysical library that he was eager to return to. The reading I received from the young woman, Kototome, was both evidential and helpful, and it inspired me to renew my spiritual search. I learned then that *one does not need to be a "believing Christian" to be of spiritual help to others.*

While in Japan, I traveled whenever I could, visiting every temple I encountered. The temple grounds were always serene and beautifully situated. Outside the entrances stood large lavers where worshippers placed sticks of burning incense, filling the air with a delightful spiritual fragrance. I often passed the Kamakura Buddha—a towering, forty-two-foot-tall bronze statue that is over a thousand years old. Simply standing before it was a spiritual experience. Within those temples, I discovered a sense of inner peace unlike anything I had known before.

When I returned to the States, I was stationed at a base in Santa Ana, California. Just an hour's drive from Hollywood, it placed me within easy reach of the Philosophical Research Society. Every Sunday, I drove in to hear the great scholar and metaphysician, Manly Palmer Hall. He could speak for an hour and a half without notes or hesitation, holding the audience in rapt attention. Among his many books was *Reincarnation: Cycle of Necessity*, which told the story of Shanti Devi, a child in 1938 India who remembered verifiable details from a previous incarnation. This case marked the beginning of my realization that reincarnation was not just a curious *belief*, but a potentially researchable *fact*.

After being discharged from the service, I enrolled at Stanford University. Several of the courses I took there made a lasting impact and deeply supported my continuing search. A class in Cultural Anthropology, taught by a husband-and-wife team of field researchers, helped crystallize my experiences in Japan. I had already seen how profoundly a culture's worldview shapes every aspect of individual life. Everything in Japan had seemed reversed—right down to how a saw cuts (upward there, downward here in the States). This course taught me that *the primacy of a culture's worldview is determinative—even of what we call fact.* Since then, I have always believed that any serious study must begin by examining the *first premise* beneath the reported facts. In a course on Goethe's *Faust,* I was warned of the dangers of seeking knowledge without the guidance of a spiritual ideal.

At the time, Stanford's psychology department was considered the best in the country, led by Robert Sears, recently arrived from Yale. I took his course on "Theories of Personality." Though our textbook covered key figures like Freud and Jung, Dr. Sears focused entirely on Stimulus-Response theory. One assignment asked us to analyze an entire Shakespeare play and demonstrate how every character's actions could be explained as an S-R sequence. This approach opened my eyes to the value of using *models* in psychological research. It became the foundation for my own model—the *Funnel*—which I would later use to explore the nature of our spiritual identity.

My favorite professor was Dr. Lee Winder, who taught Abnormal Psychology. His course laid the groundwork for my understanding of the wide range of human behavior. Stanford also allowed seniors to propose independent one-on-one research courses. Dr. Winder agreed to supervise a study I designed on hypnosis. There was a precedent: former Stanford professor Ernest Hilgard had written a book on the subject. I read everything I could find and met with Dr. Winder weekly to discuss the material. What began as a curiosity about hypnosis had now become a lifelong academic pursuit.

I also took Comparative Religion with the distinguished Professor Frederic Spiegelberg, who had just returned from a Fulbright Fellowship in India. He had published our course text, *Living Religions of the World*, and later offered a course on "The Philosophies of India." In his book *Spiritual Practices of India*, he introduced us to the *spiritual centers*, or *chakras*, which I will explore more deeply later. These studies helped prepare me for the transformative experiences I would later have during a two-week journey through India.

Through these studies, I developed a deeper appreciation for the ancient Hindu legend. In Hinduism, the most comprehensive name for God is *Brahma*. Just as in the Hebrew tradition, where "God" is rarely spoken due to its limiting connotation, *Brahma* is not to be described—but only pointed to, as *tat*, or *that*. The godhead within man is called *Atman*, or the High Self. And yet, *Brahma* and *Atman* are one and the same, as expressed in the Sanskrit phrase *tat tvam asi—that thou art*. That is, the universal principle (*Brahma*) is the same as the individual divine nature (*Atman*).

In *Beyond Theology*, Alan Watts explains why he came to prefer Hinduism over Christianity. He believed that *tat tvam asi* offered a broader, more inclusive framework than traditional Christian doctrine. But my immediate response was, *"I Am That I Am"*—God's self-revelation to Moses—embodies the same principle. When Moses asked for a name he could use to represent divine authority, the response was: *"I Am That I Am."* I understand this to mean: tell the people your inspiration comes from the *I Am*—the godhead within—which is one and the same as the *I AM*, or God without.

Dr. Spiegelberg also introduced us to Sri Aurobindo, one of India's greatest mystics and philosophers. In *Essays on the Gita*, Aurobindo describes the *Secret of Secrets*—the ultimate revelation of the *Bhagavad Gita*. In the Gita, the teacher Krishna (an incarnation of Vishnu, akin to the Christ figure) instructs the student Arjuna. At a key moment, Krishna reveals the full scope of divinity:

> All the truth that has developed itself at this length step by step, each bringing forward a fresh aspect of the integral knowledge and founding on it some result of spiritual state and action, has now to take a turn of immense importance. The Teacher therefore takes care first to draw attention to the decisive character of what he is about to say, so that the mind of Arjuna may be awakened and attentive. For he is going to open his mind to the knowledge and sight of the integral Divinity ... the Godhead in man and the world, whom nothing in man and in the world limits or binds, because all proceeds from him, is a movement in his infinite being, continues and is supported by his will, is justified in his divine self-knowledge, has him always for its origin, substance and end. Arjuna is to become aware of himself as existing only in God and as acting only by the power within him, his workings only an instrumentality of the divine action, his egotistic consciousness only a veil and to his

> ignorance a misrepresentation of the real being within him which is an immortal spark and portion of the supreme Godhead. The soul that fails to get faith in the higher truth and law must return into the path of ordinary mortal living subject to death and error and evil: it cannot grow into the Godhead which it denies. For this is a truth which has to be lived, and lived in the soul's growing light, not argued out in the mind's darkness. One has to grow into it, one has to become it - that is the only way to verify it. But, to grow thus into the freedom of the divine Nature one must accept and believe in the Godhead secret within our present limited nature.

While at Stanford, I wrote three term papers on reincarnation for different courses. I received good grades and no pushback on the subject matter. I believed it was important to be open about my views with those I would later ask for letters of recommendation.

In Palo Alto, I met Ren Rosewood, another Edgar Cayce enthusiast. Together, we formed a small *Search for God* study group. We also attended Cayce conferences in nearby San Francisco, where I heard Manly Palmer Hall speak again and was introduced to Gina Cerminara, whose book *Many Mansions* had just been published.

These experiences helped me stay grounded in my spiritual path while I navigated the academic rigors of Stanford.

I was accepted for graduate school at the University of North Carolina, where I enjoyed the friendship of two fellow graduate students: Robert Van de Castle and Charles Tart—both of whom later became experts in parapsychology. One of our psychology professors, Harold McCurdy, was also interested in the field. With my long-standing curiosity about such topics, I felt completely at home at UNC.

Just twelve miles away was Duke University, where Dr. J. B. Rhine had established his groundbreaking lab for the study of extrasensory perception. Every week, Dr. Rhine hosted a *coffee hour* around noon, where a research paper was presented and discussed. Charles Tart and I began attending these sessions regularly. I also made occasional visits to Virginia Beach, sometimes taking fellow graduate students with me.

At Stanford, I had written a term paper on children's dreams. I returned to that interest at UNC, developing a master's thesis on anxiety in children's dreams. Hugh Lynn Cayce knew of my interest and invited me to spend a summer at the Beach to study over a thousand Cayce Readings that included dream interpretations. By the end of that summer, I developed two two-week workshops on dream interpretation.

It was during this period that I came upon a dream of Cayce's in which he saw a great *funnel*—which he also referred to as a *trumpet* and a *cone*. He said that applying this vision could be helpful in understanding psychic phenomena. That fall, back in Chapel Hill, I was teaching a Sunday School class for undergraduates when one student posed a question for which I felt I could develop a helpful answer. I remembered the Cayce dream and, for the first time, drew a rough version of the *funnel* to help explain the idea. That moment marked the beginning of a framework that would shape the rest of my professional work. I call it "funnel psychology."

For the next ten years, I returned to the Beach every summer to lead dream interpretation workshops. Over time, the *funnel* model became—and remains—a central feature of my efforts to explore and explain who and what we are.

I began my Ph.D. dissertation on the topic of dream recall. My major professor told me of a member of the Department of Psychiatry who was also interested in sleep research. We developed a program to study the EEG brain wave patterns of depressed patients. So, I spent two years working in a sleep lab. I read Freud's *Interpretation of Dreams* while I observed the rapid eye movements of my dreaming subjects.

My major professor at UNC taught a course on 'Theories of Personality'. As I was finishing my degree work, he offered me the opportunity to teach the course there. This field of study continues to be a major part of my work. I became a dedicated student of these fields: Parapsychology, the Psychology of Religion, Sleep and Dreams, Personality Theory, and of course, the Bible and the Edgar Cayce Readings.

When I completed my degree, I hoped to find a teaching position at a small private university. I was fortunate to land my dream job at Trinity University in San Antonio, Texas—thanks in part to the NIMH fellowship I brought with me in sleep research, which covered my first year's salary. The School of Aerospace Medicine sponsored my work and provided access to their research facilities. One of the most formative experiences I had during my time there was attending a workshop led by the renowned psychiatrist Milton Erickson, famous for his groundbreaking approach to hypnosis.

At Trinity, I developed a course titled *Psychology and Religion*, in which we used *There Is a River* as a case study in religious experience. This course generated some controversy, but it was a deeply rewarding endeavor. I also supervised three students completing M.A. theses on parapsychological topics. During these years, I continued giving lectures and leading workshops at Virginia Beach and across the country.

Midway through the term—after nearly seven years at Trinity—I accepted an offer from Hugh Lynn to take a full-time position at the A.R.E. Just two days after arriving in Virginia Beach, I joined a group embarking on a seven-week tour around the world. We spent our first week in London meeting some of the most prominent psychics in the region: Ronald Beasley, Ursula Roberts, Ena Twig, Maurice Barbanelle, and Harry Edwards. We then traveled to Utrecht in the Netherlands to visit the famed clairvoyant Gerard Croiset. Meeting so many gifted psychics in such a short time gave me a vivid sense of how diverse psychic awareness can be.

Next, we spent a deeply spiritual week in Israel—*where Jesus walked the land and made it holy*. From there, we traveled to

India for two extraordinary weeks. In Delhi, we met a holy man named Fakir Dyal who, according to Hugh Lynn, bore the closest spiritual resemblance that he had seen to his father, Edgar Cayce. Hugh Lynn later invited him to visit Virginia Beach. When Fakir Dyal visited my own home, he gently laid his hand on the head of my three-year-old daughter. As I held her, she placed her hand on his head. I'm still not sure who received the greater blessing.

While in Rishikesh, we had an audience with the Transcendental Meditation guru, Maharishi Mahesh Yogi, at his ashram. We also met a man who recalled being a German officer—Captain Otto—during World War I. Although he was born in India, he had blonde hair with no known genetic lineage to account for it. A birthmark on his neck, he believed, marked the place where he had been fatally shot in that previous life. The doctors traveling with us examined the mark and concluded it had every appearance of a healed bullet wound. *Birthmarks are sometimes carried over from previous lives and can play a significant role in past-life research.*

We also visited Shanti Devi, whom I had previously mentioned for her childhood memories of a past life. She still recalled details from that incarnation, but what mattered most to her now was a spiritual encounter she had experienced on the spirit plane. In that vision, she met the Lord Krishna, who instructed her to return to Earth and become a spiritual teacher.

The highlight of our time in India was a visit to the Tibetan community in Dharamsala, where we spent an hour and a half with the Dalai Lama. It was a profound and unforgettable experience for all of us. He told us about his childhood memories—specifically, his being tested to determine whether he was the soul who had repeatedly incarnated as the Dalai Lama. He remembered, passed the tests, and was chosen.

From India, we traveled to Cambodia to see the great ruins of Angkor Wat. Students of reincarnation often report a feeling of *having been there before*. I certainly felt a powerful sense of remembrance in that amazing place. From there, we went to Australia to meet with Raynor Johnson, who had written several books on parapsychology, including *The Imprisoned Splendor*. Johnson was studying under a "living master" and, like many others, believed that true spiritual progress required the guidance of such a master. However, even his teacher acknowledged—*as they all do—that Jesus is the Master of masters*. As for Jesus, we may affirm with the old hymn: *"He Lives."* He is a *living Master*.

We continued on to the Fiji Islands to witness their famous firewalkers. This was a far more rigorous and authentic display than those seen in modern firewalking workshops. The participants had spent the two weeks prior in prayer and celibate seclusion. I learned then that spiritual preparation was far more essential than the more casual approaches seen in popular seminars. *Jesus taught his disciples that prayer and fasting were required for the greater spiritual manifestations.*

From Fiji, we traveled to Hawaii, where we met with several of the study groups working there.

When we returned home, while those fabulous tour experiences were still vivid in my memory, another extraordinary opportunity awaited. Hugh Lynn had been invited to attend a conference of spiritual leaders, but he chose not to go—sending me in his place.

At the conference, I had the privilege of meeting and speaking with psychics Joan Grant and Arthur Ford, along with a host of other remarkable individuals. One particularly fascinating presentation came from Clive Baxter, who described a discovery he had made using a lie detector. By attaching the device's leads to a rhododendron and *thinking* about burning the plant, he observed that the instrument recorded a response—as if the plant had sensed the threat. Joan Grant then added to the discussion by sharing her own experience of seeing plants respond to people. In a flower garden, she had witnessed plant auras reaching out to some individuals to absorb their energy, while withdrawing from others to avoid their vibrations.

Once I settled into my new job, the first major project I took on was the development of an A.R.E. meditation course. Two books came highly recommended to me: *The Secret of the Golden Flower* and *Foundations of Tibetan Mysticism* by Lama Govinda. I found both texts deeply inspiring and drew from them heavily in designing my workshops. Their teachings also became key influences in my book *Meditation and the Mind of Man*. Even now, these two works continue to shape and elevate my thinking, as in this book.

The next fourteen years at the A.R.E. were profoundly rich with opportunity. I met great teachers and writers in the field, conducted workshops all over the country, and—considering myself a researcher in the field—I received readings from every recommended psychic I could find. Many were outstanding. I delighted in studying the Readings on every imaginable subject, and sharing my insights with others. I was also featured in a nationally broadcast PBS series, *Who Is Man*, which explored parapsychology and the work of Edgar Cayce.

A highlight of that period was a trip to Russia to meet with Russian parapsychologists. Despite the stark political differences between our governments, everyone in our group was struck by how deeply similar the Russian people were to us. It was yet another reminder that *all of humankind is one family*.

During my early visits to the Beach, I met and befriended Mae Gimbert St. Clair. She had received several Readings and had occasionally lived with the Cayce family. Mae offered a rare and deeply personal understanding of Edgar Cayce and the history of the Work. We had lunch together every Tuesday for years. She worked in the Readings Research Department and would always bring a few highlighted passages—what we affectionately called "Mae's goodies"—to discuss. I could not have asked for a better education in the Readings. The richness of my experiences during those fourteen years defies explanation.

I had moved to Virginia Beach to work with Hugh Lynn, which I did for twenty-nine years. When he passed away, I was given the opportunity to reevaluate my future. I had to admit—I wasn't a perfect fit for A.R.E., and they weren't a perfect fit for me. By the grace of God, and with the help of several genuine miracles, I found myself in Phoenix: with a new job, a renewed purpose, a fresh outlook on life, and a wonderful new wife—Anne.

About ten years earlier, Anne had experienced a powerful and dramatic psychic awakening. She had always been spiritually inclined, but as a child and young adult, her psychic sensitivity revealed itself only through subtle hints. One day in a grocery store, as she browsed a rack of books, one title caught her eye. As she reached for it, a loud spirit-plane voice said, *"Buy that book."* The book was Ruth Montgomery's *A Search for the Truth.* After reading it, Anne had a full-blown psychic opening. She began to see veridical visions, to perceive auras, and to experience a profound visit with a being of light—whom she recognized as Jesus. From that moment on, she was able to offer spiritual help to others. Interestingly, although the book was life-changing when she first read it, a later rereading left her less impressed—an illustration of how we may become *conscious* of our own *growth in consciousness*.

Anne was fortunate to enroll immediately in a four-year program in metaphysical studies, focusing on psychic development. The training, offered by the National School of Spiritual Science, is something I believe should be available to all developing sensitives across the country. Soon after completing the program, she was guided to move to Phoenix—and then led to apply for a position posted by Dr. William McGarey at the A.R.E. Clinic.

Hugh Lynn had long wanted to revive the work of the Cayce Hospital, originally opened in the late 1920s. At his urging, Bill and Gladys McGarey—a husband-and-wife team of M.D.s in Phoenix—shaped their practice around treatments based on the Cayce Readings. One of the services the Clinic offered was a diagnostic psychic reading, provided by Anne, who served as Director of Spiritual Healing. People traveled from across the country and around the world to receive treatments and readings. At the time, Anne was considered one of the purest and most helpful psychics in the country. A longtime Cayce enthusiast, she worked in the same spirit and using the same method as Cayce. While her readings were less focused on vertebral subluxations—the hallmark of many Cayce readings—they often addressed *relationships* in powerful and healing ways, reflecting her more feminine spiritual energy.

When Anne and I came together, we immediately started a study group with over thirty members. We began working under the name *The Logos Center*, offering lectures and workshops around the country. I became the conductor of her readings. Over the years, I conducted more than 7,000 readings—*fully half the number given by Edgar Cayce*. I felt like the most blessed person in the world. After more than thirty years of studying the Cayce Readings, I was now working full-time with a psychic of comparable ability.

Edgar's readings would sometimes begin with an immediate observation about the client's condition—such as: *"We will continue when she stops arguing with her sister."* Hugh Lynn once checked over six hundred such comments, and *every one* proved to be accurate. I believe these comments were sometimes included to establish credibility for what followed. Anne's readings often began the same way—with a strikingly accurate observation that put the recipient on notice. We continued to work together and share with our Logos community.

Anne received spiritual guidance that we were to lead *seven* spiritual pilgrimages abroad. Our tours included 20 to 70 people and took us to Israel, Egypt, Mexico and the Yucatan, China and Tibet, Peru and Machu Picchu, and Greece and Turkey. We later returned to Israel and Egypt for our final official Logos tour. After completing those seven, we continued with additional pilgrimages to Hawaii, Greece and Turkey again, and Italy. At each holy site, we meditated together, worked with dreams, and reflected on past-life memories. We placed strong emphasis on the *spiritual history* of every sacred site. Most participants reported some sense of remembrance—an inner stirring that pointed to prior incarnations. Through these journeys, we continued to explore and deepen our understanding of the *manifestation of the Infinite into the Finite.*

Summary

Tat tvam asi! . . . that, thou art! I Am That I Am!

Since high school, I've been drawn to stories about the wisdom and accomplishments of the Tibetan lamas. A college course on comparative religion deepened that interest, prompting me to explore Buddhism—especially the often misunderstood but profoundly rich Tibetan tradition. Friends pointed me toward the writings of Lama Govinda, and his *Foundations of Tibetan Mysticism* quickly became one of the most profound and integrative works I had ever read on the subject. It offered exhilarating insights into timeless spiritual truths. I later attended a weekend workshop led by Lama Govinda to test my understanding of his work—and it was affirmed.

Although Gautama the Buddha knew the Hindu truth of *tat tvam asi*, the theology surrounding it led him to distinguish between *Atman* (the Self) and *Brahman* (the Divine). Rather than complex theological systems, Gautama urged us toward personal attunement. Through his own realization of *nirvana*, he initiated one of humanity's greatest spiritual traditions—a direct path toward self-understanding. Yet, despite his clarity, humanity has often misunderstood the teachings of its greatest spiritual figures.

Take, for example, the Buddhist goal of *nirvana*. Many imagine it as Sir Edwin Arnold famously described in *The Light of Asia*: "The dewdrop slips into the shining sea." But Lama Govinda disagrees. He believes this poetic metaphor distorts the deeper philosophical reality. Govinda writes:

If this beautiful simile is reversed, it would probably come nearer to the Buddhist conception of ultimate realization: it is not the drop that slips into the sea, but the sea that slips into the drop! The universe becomes conscious in the individual (but not vice versa), and it is in this process that completeness is achieved, in regard to which we neither can speak any more of 'individual' nor of 'universe.'

This shift—*not the drop into the sea, but the sea into the drop*—is powerful. It speaks to the Oneness of the Godhead within and the Universe without. It clarifies that our spiritual task is not simply to return to God but to *express* the fullness of God here and now.

The Edgar Cayce Readings affirm this same insight:

> Hence, as man applies himself or uses that of which he becomes conscious in the realm of activity and gives or places the credit (as would be called) in man's consciousness in the correct sphere or realm he becomes conscious of that union of force with the infinite with the finite force. Hence, in the fruits of that as is given oft, as the fruits of the spirit does man become aware of the infinite penetrating or interpenetrating the activities of all forces of matter, or that which is a manifestation of the realm of the infinite into the finite and the finite becomes conscious of same. (262-52)

The Oneness of the Divine within and without—and the direction of flow from the Infinite into the Finite—is, for me, the central theme running through the sacred texts of the world, whether Hindu, Buddhist, or Judeo-Christian. And this understanding doesn't come solely from scholarship. It arises when sacred teachings are *lived* as well as studied.

Of course, I recognize the real and sometimes irreconcilable differences between these traditions. Still, the universal message about the divine nature of humanity has always struck me as the key to grasping our shared identity as children of God. Yet the obstacles to accepting this truth are not only theological—they are deeply psychological.

Why, if this is such a universal truth, does it remain the *Secret of Secrets*? As I've said before, this is the most deeply resisted insight in all of human consciousness. To say we resist it is an understatement. When we are confronted with our divine origin, we feel anxiety—sometimes even terror. When a figure like Jesus helps us awaken to our godly nature, his presence stirs deep memory—echoes of the divine state from which we've fallen. The pain of that loss becomes unbearable. Rather than face it, we project our guilt outward as rage. We accuse the messenger of blasphemy, but psychologically, we are defending ourselves against the unbearable wound of separation.

To illustrate this, imagine a first-person encounter with Jesus, paraphrasing from John 10:30-36 (KJV):

> I and my Father are one. Then we took up stones again to stone him. Jesus answered us, many good works have I shewed you from my Father; for which of those works do ye stone me? We answered him, saying, for a good work we stone thee not; but for blasphemy; and because that thou, being a man, makest thyself God. Jesus answered us, is it not written in your law, I said, Ye are gods? If he called them gods, unto whom the word of God came, and the Scripture cannot be broken; Say ye of him, whom the Father hath sanctified, and sent into the world, thou blasphemest; because I said, I am the Son of God?

Jesus was not claiming something *exclusive* about Himself. He was reminding us, using scripture we revered, of our shared divine identity.

For me, this is one of the clearest and most powerful statements of the gospel. And it *is* good news—but not just for the intellect. It is also for the heart. The Word is not fully lived through words, but through the *love* in our hearts and the *actions* of our lives. This message belongs not to any single culture, religion, or hemisphere. It is a gift for all people.

The good news is not only that the Word was with God, the Word was God, and the Word was made flesh and dwelt among us—but also that Jesus said, "I call you not servants, but brothers and sisters."

His claim to divinity—which has become a stumbling block for many—was never about exclusion. It was about the divine origin of *every soul.* He said, *"If you have seen me, you have seen the Father."* He also said, *"I in the Father, and the Father in me, and I in you, and you in me."* That is *Oneness.*

The question of Jesus' divinity is resolved not by arguing doctrine, but by realizing that there is only *One*, and that *One is God. "Hear, O Israel, the Lord thy God is One."*

The passages I've shared, drawn from many traditions and discovered over years of searching, represent milestones in my personal quest to answer life's most profound questions: *Who are we?* and *Why are we here?*

These experiences have convinced me that we are Finite expressions of the Infinite. They encourage me to reflect with you on *A Psychology of the Soul.*

Let's continue with our work, our search, and our faith.

PART 2

A PSYCHOLOGY OF THE SOUL

CHAPTER 1
FOUNDATIONS OF OUR THINKING

"In the beginning God"—this is the most fitting and essential way to introduce any consideration of matters of ultimate importance. All human questions eventually lead back to our understanding of the Divine nature of Being. Our view of God is inseparably linked to our assumptions about the very nature of reality.

Most of us give little thought to the foundational assumptions we make about reality. We tend to accept, often uncritically, the frameworks handed to us—whether from religious traditions or the prevailing scientific paradigm. We assume that our current ways of thinking are not only sufficient, but also beyond reproach. However, history teaches us otherwise. Periodically, humanity has been required to undergo significant shifts in understanding. The Copernican revolution is a powerful example of how new discoveries can upend long-held beliefs and force us to rethink everything. Once again, we are at such a crossroads. It is time to reexamine our dominant world views and integrate newly discovered facts and deeper insights into a framework that can truly accommodate them.

We begin by asking: What is our present understanding of reality—and, by extension, of God? The challenge we face is that widely accepted world views—both religious and scientific—often reject essential facts, even those confirmed by their own systems of authority. Many Christians ignore central truths found in the Bible, just as many scientists dismiss well-documented findings from sound experimental research. These facts are not rejected because they lack credibility, but because they conflict with the assumptions that support people's preferred world views. This tendency is widespread, affecting both religious believers and scientists alike.

All world views rest upon assumptions. These foundational assumptions form our first premise, the core idea from which all other reasoning proceeds. We cannot begin with absolute facts alone because what we consider to be factual is shaped by our underlying assumptions about what reality is. If our first premise is mistaken, then all that follows will be distorted or incomplete. And indeed, both mainstream Christian theology and the prevailing scientific worldview are built on assumptions that, upon closer inspection, do not fully align with observed reality!

It is therefore necessary to reexamine the premises that underlie our thinking. Today, we primarily operate within three major world views—or theories of reality:

The Monotheistic or Theistic view, which holds that a personal God created and governs the universe.

The Scientific or Atheistic view, which assumes a universe without divine agency, governed solely by impersonal laws and chance.

The Monistic view, which posits the essential Oneness of all force and energy—often understood as consciousness or spirit manifesting as all that is.

Each of these world views begins with a basic assumption. The theistic perspective assumes a personal, purposeful Creator who imbues creation with meaning and intent. The scientific or atheistic viewpoint assumes that the universe is purely material, operating through mechanistic laws with no inherent purpose or consciousness. The monistic perspective assumes that all of reality is ultimately One—that all distinctions are manifestations of a singular underlying force or consciousness.

From these assumptions, very different interpretations of life and existence arise. The theistic view leads to a world filled with moral order and divine oversight. The scientific-atheistic view interprets existence as a series of cause-and-effect processes, often reducing human experience to biochemical and physical functions. The monistic view sees individual lives and events as expressions of a universal, interconnected Whole, sometimes referred to as the Divine, Spirit, or Consciousness.

The Cayce Readings, which will be introduced later, are deeply grounded in the monistic world view. They consistently affirm the oneness of all force. At the same time, they fully acknowledge the reality of God, the incarnations of the soul, and the purposeful evolution of consciousness. The Readings offer a unifying synthesis of these three major perspectives. They honor the theistic reverence for a loving, personal God; they respect the integrity of scientific inquiry and empirical evidence; and they assert the deep truth of our spiritual unity—that all souls are connected, and all are progressing toward the same divine fulfillment.

This integrated perspective is both liberating and challenging. It challenges us to question long-held beliefs—whether religious or scientific—and invites us to embrace a more expansive, inclusive understanding of reality. It liberates us from the either/or thinking that pits science against religion, or spirit against matter. In the Cayce view, God is both immanent and transcendent. The universe is both material and spiritual. We are both individual and one with the All.

To explore a psychology of the soul, we must begin with the recognition that all understanding is shaped by our deepest assumptions about reality. And we must be willing to revise those assumptions in the light of experience, intuition, reason, and revelation. Only then can we build a psychology that is adequate to the fullness of human experience—a psychology that honors the soul.

Monotheism

We first consider the monotheistic worldview shared by the children of Abraham: Jews, Christians, and Muslims. Monotheism is fundamentally dualistic—it posits two distinct kinds of reality: God, and material existence. In this view, materiality is not seen as an emanation from God but rather as something created *ex nihilo*, or "out of nothing." This theory of creation places God outside of the physical universe. The physical world, in turn, is thought to be governed by "natural law," and divine action within it is considered a miraculous intervention—something rare and extraordinary that suspends the ordinary operation of these laws.

This perspective tends to distance God from daily life, portraying divine involvement as infrequent, remote, and even arbitrary. For those who believe in prayer, this framework poses a challenge: one must summon enough faith to persuade God to intervene. This sometimes leads believers to wonder why God hasn't already acted. If God is both all-powerful and all-loving, how can suffering and evil persist? Why must we plead for divine help when such issues seem to call for automatic compassion and response?

These are not abstract questions—they are deeply personal and often troubling. After the Oklahoma City bombing in 1995, where 168 people were killed, evangelist Billy Graham remarked that he could not understand why God allows such tragedies. His reaction reflected a theological void: Christian doctrine, as traditionally taught, provides no framework for understanding such events if God is assumed to be outside the world and capable of intervening at will. If so, why, then, does He not act?

Billy Graham was a powerful preacher and a man of deep faith, but he was not schooled in the universal laws that govern soul development—laws which suggest that the soul's journey toward oneness with the Father spans eons, not moments. In the traditional Christian view, the soul's path is reduced to a simple duality: we die and go to either heaven or hell. Yes it is not that simple, nor is it biblical. For as Jesus said, "...strait is the gate, and narrow is the way, which leadeth unto life, and few there be that find it" (Matt. 7:14). The complexity of that journey, and the effort required, are far greater than commonly preached.

Indeed, a half-truth can be more dangerous than a full lie. While Christian teaching may inspire many to dedicate their lives to Christ—undoubtedly a good thing—it can also breed complacency. Some believe that once they are "saved," their spiritual work on themselves is done. The need for deeper seeking may be shelved indefinitely, even while their lives remain unchanged in meaningful ways.

Monotheism also requires us to view humanity strictly as a creation—mere creatures. This assumption stands in conflict with numerous biblical passages asserting that we are "...gods, children of the most High." (Psalm 82:6). Still, Christian theologians cling to the *ex nihilo* premise, despite the absence of any biblical verse to support it—and despite the presence of many verses that suggest otherwise.

Anthropologists studying various cultures have noted a troubling pattern: societies that place Spirit or God outside of nature—as monotheism does—tend to be more warlike and exploitative. History, tragically, affirms this tendency among all of the major monotheistic traditions.

The Scientific World View

Second, we consider the so-called "scientific" worldview. Motivated by legitimate concerns about the arbitrary nature of "divine intervention" and a rightful desire to affirm the lawfulness of natural processes, a group of bright students in 1845 began to argue that natural law alone was sufficient to explain the workings of both the universe and human beings. These students were disciples of the renowned physiologist Johannes Müller, and they banded together to oppose *vitalism*—the belief that life involves forces beyond those found in inorganic matter. They rejected concepts such as *élan vital* or any notion of a "life force."

For these thinkers, the very idea of God was not only deemed unnecessary, it was seen as fundamentally incompatible with the goals of scientific inquiry. Just thirty-five years later, this anti-vitalist stance had become the prevailing view throughout the scientific community.

However, the major flaw in this worldview is that it is, ironically, not truly scientific. It functions as a closed system—closed to certain types of data and to entire fields of inquiry. For instance, this worldview categorically dismisses results from parapsychological research, despite the fact that such research is rigorously conducted and scientifically validated. Parapsychology is the systematic study of phenomena like telepathy, clairvoyance, and precognition. These phenomena, demonstrated through repeatable experiments, strongly suggest that our current understanding of physical law is too limited—and fundamentally flawed.

What is most striking is the depth of emotional resistance to this research, particularly among two seemingly opposed groups: atheistic scientists and "ex nihilo" Christians. Both camps tend to react not with curiosity or critique, but with anger—even when simply confronted with the topic. Their response is often not based on rational analysis of the data, but rather on an emotional rejection of what that data might imply. This resistance reveals a phenomenon we might call "preferred ignorance"—a willful disregard for uncomfortable facts.

The pursuit of so-called "scientific respectability" too often suppresses the very spirit of open inquiry that has driven scientific progress for centuries. When evidence that challenges foundational assumptions is ignored or dismissed out of hand, science ceases to be a method for discovery and becomes instead a dogma of denial.

Monism

The third worldview has existed throughout human history and is now entering into broader awareness. This is the understanding that there is only God. It is referred to as a monistic worldview. Monism affirms Oneness—the idea that there is only one force, one substance, in the universe. *Everything is God.* And, for emphasis, we might say that *every non-thing* is God. That is, all that is manifest and all that is un-manifest is God. All that is immanent and all that is transcendent is God. Thus, the monistic worldview is grounded in the assumption of the Oneness of all force. And what is this one force?

The most meaningful and inclusive answer may be: God. As the Apostle Paul proclaimed from a consciousness of Oneness: "For in him we live, and move, and have our being." (Acts 17:28)

The great affirmation of the ancient Israelites, the Shema, declares: "Hear, O Israel: The Lord thy God is one Lord; there is none other." In Hebrew, the word *ein* translated as "none" may also be rendered "nothing." Thus, the Shema may be understood as affirming not only that there is no other God, but that there is *nothing other than God.* Jewish mystics have long embraced this second, equally valid—and arguably more revealing—translation: There is one God, and there is nothing other than God.

The teachings of Jesus cannot be fully understood apart from this consciousness of Oneness. He said: "I in you, you in me, and I in the Father." That is Oneness.

One of the earliest and most influential Western proponents of Oneness was the 17th-century Jewish philosopher Baruch

Spinoza. He argued that there is only one substance in the universe. Whether we call it Nature, the Universe, Being, or God, Spinoza maintained, the name does not change its essence. The idea of Oneness, then, is not new, nor is it a fringe import from Eastern traditions—it has deep roots in Judaism.

It is impossible to prove which of the three basic assumptions—theistic, atheistic, or monistic—is ultimately correct. But we can gather compelling evidence in support of each. For example, consider Einstein's famous equation: $E = mc^2$. Universally accepted as accurate, this equation may be interpreted through the lens of Oneness: let E, energy, represent Spirit, and M, mass, represent materiality. The equation suggests that mass can be converted into energy, and energy can be manifested as mass. Given that, then the only distinction between Spirit and matter is the rate and quality of vibration.

Modern developments in quantum theory lend further support to the monistic view. Physicist Alan Boyles, for instance, has argued that there is no such thing as empty space. His research on quantum vacuum theory explores the deep-field potentiality that underlies all manifest phenomena. To illustrate, consider the states of water—it may be solid, liquid, or gas. In its gaseous form, it resembles Spirit, which, as Jesus said, "listeth where it will."

The monistic worldview also resolves the persistent theological dilemma in the ex nihilo doctrines of the Abrahamic religions: the separation between God and humankind. Our understanding of Oneness may be limited while we inhabit this three-dimensional earthly plane. And yet, we can use 3-D concepts to gain a clearer view. God is One, but we may better comprehend God through the triune understanding: Father, Son, and Holy Spirit. Similarly, time is conceived as past, present, and future; space as height, length, and breadth; humankind as spiritual, mental, and physical. The human body is likewise understood as having spiritual, mental, and physical components, and consciousness itself as superconscious, subconscious, and conscious.

All of these are *One*, expressed in threefold aspects. It is like understanding a box—not as separate sides, but as one object with three dimensions: length, width, and height. The Cayce Readings describe these dimensions as *Time, Space,* and *Patience.* Everett Irion, a student of the Readings, further explained: Time is the measure of our understanding of an idea; Space is the measure of our understanding of a manifest idea; and Patience is the measure of our understanding of the purpose of a manifest idea.

For example, consider a mother preparing a birthday cake for her child. She has a recipe—an idea. But not everyone with a recipe can produce a good cake—a manifest idea. Her intention is to bring joy to her child. But if, in the process, the child misbehaves and she becomes impatient, she may forget her purpose. In this case, Patience helps her stay grounded in intention. We might say that Patience is the understanding that: *things are the way they are for a reason.*

So, what may we affirm about the nature of God? God is not a person—certainly not three persons—but we can have a personal relationship with Him. When we call God "Him" or "Father," we are not designating gender, but the nature of relationship. If I call a friend "brother," I speak to the bond between us, not a biological or familial tie.

We may speak of polarities—positive and negative—not in terms of gender but of energy. Thus, we might say Father/Mother God to signify both poles of Divine Being. In fact, the Cayce Readings occasionally refer to the Father/Mother God in Jesus.

God is Spirit. God is Universal Consciousness. God is Beingness. God is Lawful. God is Intelligence. And God is Love.

Love is lawful, and lawfulness is an attribute of Love. We know that lawfulness is more loving than chaos. And we may know something about God because we are God's children—god beings. God is both Love and Law. Emphasizing one or the other depends on the context of our concern.

We might visualize two lines: one representing *Love*, the other *Law*. They may also be seen as *Grace* and *Karma*. In the Sermon on the Mount, Jesus shifts the emphasis from the Old Testament's Law to His own Law of Grace. Every time He says, "You have heard it said ... but I say unto you," He shifts from an emphasis on Law to an emphasis on Grace. In doing so, He moves us from the Law of Karma to the Law of Love, one expression of which is the Great Commandment. God is love, and all of His laws, properly understood, are laws of Love and Grace.

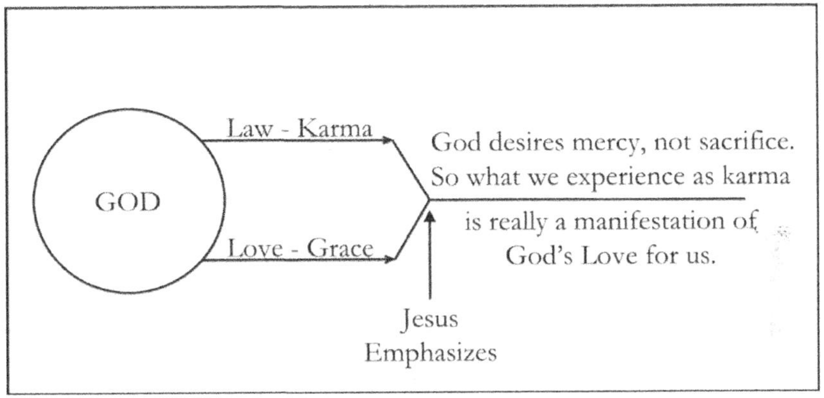

Figure 1: Shifting from Karma to Grace Is a Matter of Emphasis

The proper understanding of what is called karma is that it is a manifestation of God's Love. There are clearly things we do that are not loving. Jesus is saying that God's love is seeking to redirect those things. We call it karma because we don't understand that God's chastening of us is an aspect of His love. We may have painful experiences and call them karmic with a negative connotation. But like any good father that is preventing his children from making choices that are not in their best interest, it is actually an act of a love.

There are Universal Laws—immutable, inflexible, and consistent. These laws operate on the physical, mental, and spiritual levels of experience. What we call "miracles" are, in truth, the application of higher spiritual laws. Our failure to recognize these laws stems largely from the worldviews in which we are immersed—worldviews that ignore or deny the spiritual dimension of law. And yet, some spiritual laws may be more exacting than physical ones.

With these reflections on first premises and worldviews complete, we now turn our attention to the nature of the soul.

The Soul

Some wise individuals have said that we don't have a soul—we *are* a soul. Unfortunately, most people respond to this profound idea not with curiosity but with silence, as if it were the end of a discussion rather than the beginning. But it should invite our deepest inquiry. What can we learn about the soul?

The psychic work of Edgar Cayce, known as the Readings, provides remarkable insight into this question. As "gods, children of the most High" (Ps. 82), we are god-beings within the Beingness of God. As such, we are souls made in the image of God—eternal beings without beginning or end. The Readings describe the soul as a facet, a characteristic, a corpuscle, a love in the body of God. There is nothing in the Universe—or in the Beingness of God—that does not have its reflection within us. We begin to understand this more fully as we grasp the body's purpose as a Temple. The soul is our spiritual body—our true being. The subconscious is the mind of the soul. This soul-mind is eternal and indestructible, and it expresses without limitation when it operates in harmony with the Law of Love.

As co-creators in three-dimensional existence, our souls are endowed with minds, with which to build; wills, with which to choose; and access to the one force—Spirit—through which we may manifest what we envision. Mind is the builder, and so long as our intentions, decisions, and creations align with the Law of Love, the soul's creative power is limitless. When we are incarnate, the mind of the soul functions as the subconscious mind. When we are not in the body, that subconscious becomes the conscious mind, which retains the entire history and memory of the soul from its creation.

Oneness with God was our original state. And in God's love, Oneness is also our final destiny. This Oneness means full attunement and harmony with God and the Law of Love. The Master's parable of the prodigal son is the soul's story. We were once one with God. We strayed of our own will, even while still celestial beings. That choice led us away, and now, recognizing how things have gone, we begin to say as did the prodigal, "I will arise and return to my Father." When we consider the Master's affirmation that we are gods and His siblings, we can begin to grasp the lawfulness behind the conditions of our lives.

Personhood

The Christian theory of "personhood" beginning at conception is deeply problematic and not biblically grounded. Genesis 2:7 tells us, "...the Lord God formed man of the dust of the ground and breathed into his nostrils the breath of life; and man became a living soul." It is clear: no nostrils, no breath—no breath, no soul. Genesis 7 clearly affirms that life is defined by breath in the nostrils.

The Readings state that the soul enters at or shortly after the first breath. This has significant implications for the abortion debate. I once heard TV preacher John Hagee assert, “This is what the Bible says about abortion.” But what does the Bible actually say?

> “If men strive, and hurt a woman with child, so that her fruit depart from her, and yet no mischief follow: he shall surely be punished, according as the woman’s husband will lay upon him; and he shall pay as the judges determine. And if any mischief follow, then thou shalt give life for life, eye for eye, tooth for tooth, hand for hand, foot for foot.” (Ex. 21:22–24)

This passage appears in chapter 21, just after the Ten Commandments in chapter 20. In the same chapter 21, we also read: “Whoever strikes father or mother shall be put to death” (v.15) and “Whoever curses father or mother shall be put to death” (v.17, NRSV). Apparently, in those times—when barrenness was considered a curse—the miscarriage of a fetus, even due to violence, was not treated with the same gravity. The God of the Ten Commandments did not issue the severest penalties for such cases. Back then, a man could cause a miscarriage and not be accused of murder. Yet one could be put to death for much less cause. Nowadays good Christians can curse their parents without consequence.

If the belief systems of a church wishes to teach its members to oppose abortion, it has every right to do so. But to extend that doctrine to the laws of a nation—or the world—is simply not justified by the Bible. An abortion, in spiritual terms, deprives a waiting soul of the chance to incarnate at that moment. But that soul may return later, perhaps through the same mother, under more favorable circumstances—such as through a beloved husband rather than through a rapist.

The real question is not when life begins. It is: what right do the government or the church have to tell a woman what she must do with the processes of her own body? I do not believe that most politicians who vote to oppose abortion care about the issue itself. They are motivated by the desire to please the nation's largest voting bloc—without which they would not stay in office.

The Readings also offer profound guidance for prospective parents on how to prepare themselves as channels for incoming souls. At the moment of conception, the ideals of the parents determine the type of soul that will be drawn to them. When guided by spiritual intention, they may attract very high souls. This has great significance for the spiritual advancement of the world. With the incarnation of advanced souls, the planet may be better prepared for the eventual return of more wayward souls under improved conditions. This, the Readings say, is the purpose behind the prophesied one thousand years of peace.

Contrary to modern theories, the Readings teach that from the beginning, souls entered human bodies at five different locations and in five distinct races, all at the same time. These five races correspond to the five senses, suggesting that each sensory emphasis contributes uniquely to the soul's journey toward universal awareness. Perhaps, for the white race, the emphasis is on vision; for the black race, on audition. It is undeniable that Black Americans have made a major and lasting contribution to the sacred music of this country.

Continuity and Karma

As pre-existing souls—co-creators with God and endowed with free will—we begin to see more clearly how we are responsible for the circumstances and conditions of our lives. The plainly stated Biblical truths that "what we sow, we will reap" and that "like begets like" are not merely moral suggestions but immutable laws. To understand how these laws operate, we must recognize both the preexistence and the continuity of the soul's life. If we reap what we sow, then what we are experiencing now must have been sown previously—whether in this lifetime or in one before. Likewise, what we are sowing now, we will eventually reap—if not in this life, then in a future one. This single insight resolves countless questions that the limited perspectives of atheism and theism cannot even begin to answer. It is a direct application of the law: like begets like.

There are numerous affirmations of this law throughout the New Testament. Jesus teaches, "If you live by the sword, you will die by the sword." On two occasions, He tells us that the prophecy of Elijah's return—given in Malachi—was fulfilled in John the Baptist. Elijah, it is recorded, killed 450 priests of

Baal with a sword. John the Baptist was himself beheaded. (See Malachi 4:5; Matthew 11:10–15; 1 Kings 18:40, 19:1). The principle of cause and effect unfolds across lifetimes; it may take hundreds of years, but the law will be fulfilled. As Jesus said, "Heaven and earth shall pass away, but my words shall not pass away" (Matthew 24:35). Clearly, Jesus was teaching the law of karma—and it is only through the lens of reincarnation that this law can be fully understood. I explore this teaching in greater depth in my book, *Why Jesus Taught Reincarnation.*

This world view—the Oneness of all force—as a foundational premise allows for a deeper and more meaningful interpretation of the Bible. It opens the door to integrating spiritual and mental laws with the scientific understanding of physical laws. As this world view becomes more widely accepted, it will enrich our understanding of the soul's journey and the greater purpose of life on Earth. Yet, such a paradigm shift inevitably meets resistance. It challenges long-held traditions, entrenched dogmas, and vested interests. And as history shows, the greater the truth revealed, the greater the opposition it provokes.

Our Search for The Truth

In our search for truth, we have traditionally turned to two primary sources: Science and Religion. These serve as the foundations of our understanding—of ourselves and of the world around us. From them, we seek not only what is true, but also what is meaningful and important. Science offers truth through the correlation of objective observations, experimental research, the discovery of laws, and the application of those laws. Religion, on the other hand, draws upon divine inspiration—often through prophets—or from religious traditions rooted in the teachings of revered spiritual figures.

Let's consider Science. What can this great discipline justifiably claim as truth? What we call "science" today actually involves two distinct components: the **scientific method** and the **scientific world view**. The scientific method is a powerful and fruitful process of discovery. In contrast, the scientific world view is a philosophical framework—often under-examined—that imposes artificial limits on inquiry. Many of science's current claims and prejudices arise more from allegiance to this philosophical assumption than from empirically derived data. Because the scientific method and the scientific world view developed historically in parallel, they are often mistaken as inseparable. But they are not. In fact, when scientific findings conflict with this established world view, the world view is often given preference—even at the cost of dismissing valid experimental data. This is not true science. Unfortunately, this very problem has occurred repeatedly with the findings of parapsychology.

Parapsychology is the scientific study of psychic phenomena, including intuition, telepathy, clairvoyance, precognition, and psychokinesis. These are referred to in the Bible as "the gifts of the Spirit" (1 Corinthians 12). The broader field of psychical research also encompasses the study of out-of-body experiences, communication with the spirit plane, dowsing, prayer, spiritual healing, the survival of the soul after death, and reincarnation.

These subjects are not difficult to research. In fact, many of these phenomena are far more measurable and repeatable than effects observed in fields such as astronomy or quantum physics. Psychic phenomena lend themselves to rigorous experimentation. Even a high school science student could design and carry out a meaningful study in this area.

One striking example is the evidence for reincarnation, which has been documented in thousands of cases where children recall specific, verifiable details from past lives. Any single one of these cases should be enough to convince an open and seeking mind of the factual reality of reincarnation. The body of evidence is vast and accessible, yet opponents and skeptics often reduce reincarnation to a mere "belief"—something curious or exotic—instead of treating it as a demonstrable fact. Either it works this way, or it doesn't. The available evidence overwhelmingly supports the former. Facts, when honestly evaluated, should prompt us to reconsider our beliefs. Yet many people still hold to their views in spite of the evidence, as in the old joke: "My mind is made up! Don't confuse me with the facts."

When our beliefs are contradicted by well-established facts, then no matter how deeply we cherish those beliefs, we are obligated to reexamine and—if necessary—revise them.

Science as A Biped

The nature of scientific progress was insightfully explored by James Conant, former president of Harvard University, in his essay *On Understanding Science*. Conant proposed that science advances like a biped, taking two essential steps. First, data must be gathered through objective observation and rigorous study. Second, these data must be integrated into a conceptual theory—one that accounts for *all* of the findings. If a theory cannot accommodate the complete set of facts, it must be revised, expanded, or replaced. An adequate theory should also generate new research questions, leading to new hypotheses and further experimentation. In turn, these investigations may yield new data that require the conceptual framework to evolve again.

The principle is straightforward: gather the facts, formulate a theory that explains them and prompts new inquiry, then revise or replace the theory as needed. According to Conant, if new data are collected but no new or adjusted theory follows, then no real scientific progress has been made. Science, like a walker, must take both steps—data collection and theoretical innovation—or it ceases to move forward.

In the field of parapsychology, the first step has already been taken—repeatedly and successfully—through well-documented, peer-reviewed studies. Since J.B. Rhine published his seminal book *ESP* in 1933, hundreds of experiments have confirmed the existence of psychic phenomena such as telepathy, clairvoyance, and precognition. By all conventional scientific standards, the body of evidence is sufficient for serious acceptance. Yet, progress is blocked because the findings challenge the prevailing scientific world view. The second step—updating the theoretical framework to account for these results—is routinely ignored.

When scientists refuse to revise their theories in the face of compelling data, they reveal a loss of objectivity. In many cases, they are protecting a vested interest in maintaining outdated models—or expressing an emotional bias against what the implications of new data might mean. The outcome is predictable: entire areas of human experience, particularly those related to consciousness and psychic functioning, are dismissed as "non-scientific." Even conducting research in these fields can be viewed as lacking "scientific respectability."

As previously stated, this attitude amounts to preferred ignorance—the willful dismissal of legitimate data because it threatens deeply held assumptions. As a result, whether we search for truth through Christianity or through Science, our pursuit can be obstructed by entrenched dogmatism. The American Psychological Association once published a special issue on intuition, yet astonishingly failed to include a single reference to the vast body of research in parapsychology.

It is now necessary to affirm that there *is* a persistent bias embedded in the modern scientific world view—one that acts as a barrier to discovery. If we limit our investigation to what is permissible within the bounds of classical physics, we exclude vast dimensions of human experience that fall outside materialist assumptions. Findings from decades of reputable research in parapsychology are often met not with scientific skepticism, but with outright hostility. Critics frequently claim there is "no convincing scientific evidence," or worse, that the results must have been faked—accusations made without examining the actual data.

This resistance stems not from the scientific method but from unwavering loyalty to a worldview that cannot accommodate the data. In *The Book: On the Taboo Against Knowing Who You Are*, philosopher Alan Watts aptly described this phenomenon as a taboo—an unspoken prohibition against exploring who and what we truly are. It is this taboo, masked as scientific skepticism, that must be overcome if we are to move forward in our search for truth.

Science and The Bible

The evidence clearly demonstrates the inadequacy—and the fundamental flaw—of the world view that relies solely on the "known" laws of physics. Ironically, many Christians reject the verified findings of parapsychology as heretical, despite the fact that this body of scientific data actually supports numerous so-called "miracles" described in the Bible. For example, understanding the principles of psychokinesis offers a plausible framework for how Elisha caused a sunken axe head to float (2 Kings 6:5–7).

Unfortunately, most Christians have conceded to the scientific community's denial of such events, believing that science has disproven their possibility. This mindset has resulted in a loss of faith and a weakened pursuit of biblical truth. A striking example is the 1960s "Death of God" movement, which emerged from the mistaken belief that science had proven the nonexistence of God. Even public education systems have embraced this scientific materialism—refusing to teach anything outside of atheistic Darwinism. Intelligent design is categorically excluded. In their attempt to avoid religion, they have instead chosen ignorance. Discussion of God need not be purely religious; it can also be a rational conversation about facts and truth. Observing the lawful operations of nature does not rule out the presence of a Divine intelligence behind them.

Consider Stephen Hawking, widely regarded as one of the most brilliant minds of the 20th century. Hawking was a strict determinist, convinced that within nanoseconds of the "Big Bang," the future of the universe—including every event—was set irreversibly in motion. This extreme view was fully consistent with, and required by, his atheistic world view. If one assumes that all phenomena must conform to currently known physical laws, then Hawking's determinism is logical. But this is scientism—not science. Very few people, even among scientists, truly believe that we lack free will or the ability to choose. Yet, if we do possess free will, it implies that we are more than physical bodies. Indeed, are souls—spiritual beings.

Psychologists have long struggled to construct theories of free will that exclude the concept of the soul, and none have been convincing. Free will remains one of our most cherished human capacities. Attempts by defense attorneys to argue that criminals are not responsible for their actions—because science has shown behavior to be predetermined—have posed serious threats to the integrity of the justice system. These arguments have rightly been rejected.

The materialist world view fails to address life's most meaningful aspects: love, altruism, creativity, empathy, emotion, and personal responsibility. Most significantly, it fails to explain *life itself*—and that most treasured phenomenon of all: consciousness. In fact, materialist science dismisses consciousness as an “epiphenomenon”—a byproduct of physical processes for which it offers no real explanation. In other words, consciousness “just happened,” an inexplicable side effect in a universe that, by this view, has no soul.

Once again, we see that the so-called scientific world view is not truly scientific—it is a set of limiting assumptions. It discourages curiosity, stifles discovery, and restricts inquiry. It assumes, without evidence, that there is no God, and refuses to consider any truth that falls outside its narrow framework. Science must assume that the universe is lawful—but we must also allow that there are laws we do not yet understand, and forces we have not yet recognized. To claim otherwise is not science; it is dogma.

The error lies in the historical influence of Christian theology, which placed God *outside* of the physical universe—claiming that in order for God to act, He must suspend or override His own natural laws. In response, atheists have rightly rejected this model, preferring instead a view of universal lawfulness. Yet they go further, without justification, by asserting that *all* causation must be accounted for by *only* those laws known to current physics. There is no scientific basis for this assumption.

We must overcome the widespread “preferred ignorance” of those who cling to outdated, unsupported world views. Science has not proven that biblical events such as healings, levitations, or prophecy could not have happened. In fact, the history of science is filled with examples of once-dismissed ideas becoming widely accepted. Who in 1899 would have believed in the possibility of the Boeing 747? Yet 70 years later, we had a 455-ton aircraft traveling halfway around the globe, cruising five miles above Earth at nearly the speed of sound, carrying 300 people in comfort and safety—all made possible by the laws of aerodynamics. And even that achievement now pales in comparison to space travel and the latest research into the fundamental nature of reality.

Today, we stand at the threshold of another great leap forward—much like the Wright brothers in 1903. We must be careful about labeling anything "impossible." In 1947, my high school physics teacher told the class that sending a man to the moon was entirely feasible. When I told my father, he laughed and said, "That's impossible." Years later, when I shared my growing interest in parapsychology, he replied, "Well, I know better than to say something is impossible!" We should all adopt that wisdom: we should all "know better."

In our search for truth, we must stop treating science as a sacred cow, immune to challenge. We should marvel at the accomplishments of the physical sciences—but also recognize the promise of new discoveries in equally significant dimensions. Parapsychology has demonstrated that the spiritual and mental realms are governed by lawful principles that can be studied and applied—just like physical laws. As we learn to explore and harness these laws, we may come to understand how walking on water, restoring sight, and even raising the dead were not violations of nature, but demonstrations of mastery over physical, mental, and spiritual law.

Lawfulness

At the heart of true science lies the discovery and application of the laws that govern observed events. This foundational principle is what gives science its power and reliability. Isaac Newton is still regarded by many as the greatest scientist of all time precisely because he identified and articulated the underlying lawfulness of physical phenomena. It is also significant that Newton was a spiritual seeker, recognizing the unity between the laws of nature and the divine.

To affirm the principle of lawfulness is to accept that, as god beings and co-creators with God, we are responsible for the conditions of our lives. The question is not, "Why doesn't God fix this?" but rather, "What can we learn about ourselves through the choices that have lawfully led to these present circumstances?" The universal law that like begets like cannot be denied. In the biblical tradition, this is stated simply: "We reap what we sow."

To fully grasp the implications of this law, one must accept the pre-existence of the soul. Reincarnation becomes a necessary framework for understanding the long-term consequences of our choices across lifetimes. This is not mere speculation but is supported by substantial empirical evidence. For example, Dr.

Ian Stevenson's extensive research at the University of Virginia includes thousands of meticulously documented cases of

children who remember past lives. One particularly compelling account is found in *Soul Survivor: The Reincarnation of a World War II Fighter Pilot*, written by Bruce and Andrea Leininger, the parents of a young boy whose detailed memories of a past life are too precise to dismiss. Anyone who reads this case with an open mind will find it difficult to deny the factual basis for reincarnation.

Instead of resenting God or blaming others for the suffering we see in the world, we are invited to take a deeper view: that we are not passive victims, but active participants in shaping our own realities. If the law is that like begets like, then the circumstances we face are not divine punishments or arbitrary misfortunes, but the lawful consequences of our own choices—often made long before our current incarnation.

Recognizing ourselves as eternal souls with free will empowers us to shift perspective. Our challenges can become stepping-stones instead of stumbling blocks. Do we choose to blame others, or do we accept the responsibility to grow, to learn, and to evolve? Our emotional and psychological well-being—our mental hygiene—depends on whether we assume responsibility for our current situation or continue to project blame outward. If "they" are responsible, then "they" must change. But when we take responsibility for ourselves, we can align more fully with the Universal Law of Love. This alignment sets us on the path to true soul development.

We must no longer accept the limiting beliefs and willful ignorance promoted by both traditional theism and rigid atheism. Like the Prodigal Son, we are called to awaken to our divine heritage, to rise, and to reclaim our birthright as "gods, children of the Most High." As we embrace the world view of Oneness, we open ourselves to a richer understanding of who we are and why we are here.

Our understanding of ourselves as souls requires a study of the spiritual functions of the endocrine system, for in this we will find "the seat of the soul."

The Lord's Prayer and the Seven Centers

As we move forward, it is essential that we consider the importance of the relationship between the seven spiritual centers and the words of the Lord's Prayer.

The Glad Helpers healing group (a special Cayce study group) asked:

> Q-22 Does the Lord's prayer have any bearing on the opening of the centers?
> A-22 Here is indicated the manner in which it was given (and) the purpose for which it was given.
>
> Q-23 Pituitary – Heaven?
> A-23 Correct. In all of its activities these open, for the upward lift of the thoughts of man as in relationships to that which becomes – how has it been given? – "He is alpha, omega, the beginning and end." Hence as we find in its relationships to man, it becomes then the

beginnings, the endings, of all things. [The Pituitary is the broadcasting center for prayer.]

Q-24 Pineal – Name?
A-24 … yes.

Q-25 Thyroid – Will?
A-25 Correct.

Q-26 Thymus – Evil?
A-26 Correct.

Q-27 Solar Plexus – Debts?
A-27 Correct.

Q-28 Lyden – Temptation?
A-28 Correct.

Q-29 Gonads – Bread?
A-29 Right.

Q-30 How should the Lord's Prayer be used in this connection?
A-30 As in feeling, as it were, the flow of the meanings of each portion of same throughout the body-physical. For as there is the response to the mental representations of all of these in the *mental* body, it may build into the physical body in the manner as He, thy Lord, thy Brother, so well expressed in, "I have bread ye know not of."

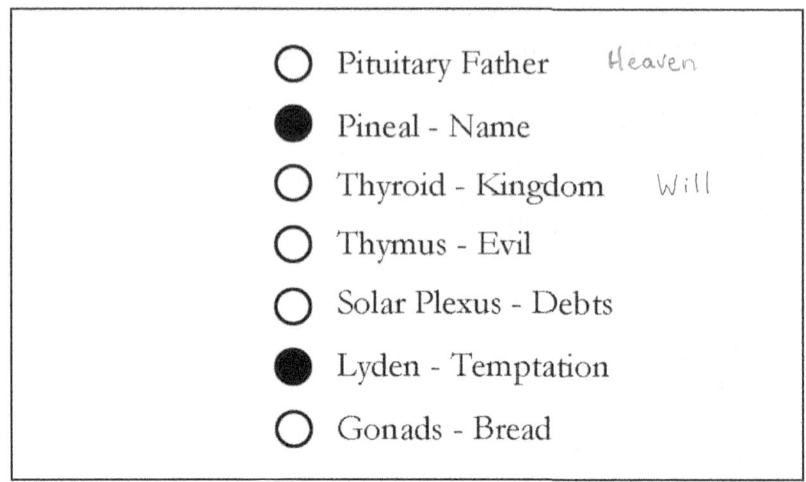

Figure 2: Each Line of the Lord's Prayer Is Directed To Clear a Specific Center

Figure 2 is a step toward understanding spiritual laws. The Lord's prayer says: "Our Father which art in Heaven, Hallowed be Thy Name …"

When we pray "in His name," we may think by uttering this phrase that we have guarantee that the prayer will surely be answered. But this doesn't seem to work so well. We *must* raise the forces to the pineal, the Christ Center. So, as we pray with intention, breathing normally through the nose, we can visualize or imagine life-force energies being drawn from the lower centers to the higher ones. This is the Name within this process by which our prayers are empowered and that is where the magic happens.

We close the prayer with: "for Thine is the kingdom (thyroid), the power (pineal) and the glory (pituitary)." When we say, there is power in the blood, this the internal process of when the kundalini rises and activates the pineal, then the hormonal secretions, (which I refer to as an elixir) enliven, cleanse and empower the other centers, thus: "there is power in the blood." This is symbolized in the Bible.

In the OT worship there were animal sacrifices such as a bull or pigeons. This relates to the four beasts of the Revelation. The sacrificial bull is represented in the calf of the four beasts. As the calf bows down in the Revelation, it represents the OT sacrifice of the bull. This represents the release of the first center energies for the rising of the kundalini energies. As it rises the other centers bow, such as the eagle of the fourth center. This is like the sacrifice of the pigeons representing the fourth center.

Thus we see clarification of scripture implying that God does not desire sacrifice. The OT sacrifices were simply emblematic of the process that must occur during meditation.

Chapter 2
Psychics, Parapsychology and Psychical Research

The Edgar Cayce Story

The story of the life and work of Edgar Cayce may well be—second only to the life and work of Jesus—*"the greatest story ever told."* Cayce was, on the surface, an ordinary man. Yet he was also a profoundly gifted soul, endowed with a deep spiritual ability and unwavering dedication. He served as the humblest of messengers, often overlooked—much like our own still, small voice or our neglected dreams.

Cayce's greatness lies in a life devoted to selfless service. His work is best understood as a channel for the expression of Universal Consciousness—a term that is, in essence, synonymous with the force and awareness we call God.

This work was commonly referred to as "giving Readings." These were spiritual discourses delivered in an unconscious response to questions posed by thousands of seekers who came to Cayce for guidance. The topics they raised spanned nearly the full range of human experience. As these discourses were transcribed, compiled, and studied, they became a source of profound inspiration and insight—potentially capable of ushering in the greatest good the world has ever known.

This potential exists because Cayce's work is a continuation of the work of Jesus, who became the Christ. Cayce himself did not explicitly frame his work this way, as even the word Christ can seem limiting to some. The information he shared is universal in its scope and application. Many Christians believe divine revelation ended with the final words of the last book in the Bible—Revelation. But why would this be so? There is no solid reason to believe it. The warning not to add or subtract from that book applies only to the book itself. It was, after all, written well before it became the Bible's final entry.

Our readiness to receive truth has long been an obstacle. This is illustrated in several ways. Jesus said plainly: "I have many things to tell you, but you cannot receive them now." The apostle Paul criticized his followers for needing spiritual "milk" when they should have been ready for "meat." The author of Hebrews lamented that his audience was too "dull of hearing" to grasp deeper insights about Melchizedek. In the Old Testament, the people begged their prophets to "prophesy to us smooth things." And Jesus Himself rebuked the people for their habit of killing their prophets because they were unwilling to hear the truth.

It is telling that *every* field of study recognizes that we still have much to learn—except, it seems, for religion, and especially Christianity. In Cayce's Readings, we find that the truths of the Bible are not only affirmed but expanded for greater understanding. And we still have much to learn—and unlearn. Often, unlearning proves the greater challenge. How many times have we heard someone say, "Well, I've always believed that…"? We tend to cling tightly to old, cherished beliefs, even when they no longer serve us.

There are several biographies, hundreds of books, and thousands of articles about Cayce and his work. Among them, the most comprehensive is Sidney Kirkpatrick's *Edgar Cayce: An American Prophet*. The accuracy and usefulness of Cayce's Readings have been documented so thoroughly that they form a mountain of evidence—virtually incontrovertible in what they reveal. Thomas Sugrue's *There Is a River* offers a beautiful account of Cayce's extraordinary life. The final chapter of that book provides a particularly rich summary of Cayce's philosophy. And yet, despite all this, there remains something of a conspiracy of silence among mainstream sources. They celebrate the work of far lesser figures while overlooking Cayce's profound contributions.

Consider one simple example. The Cayce Source suggested that eating a few almonds each day could help prevent the body's tendency to develop cancers or tumors. That's not a statement of faith—it's a hypothesis, and one easily tested. Even if this approach helped just 10 percent of cancer cases, the result would be a dramatic reduction in suffering and a massive saving of lives and resources. Why isn't this being studied? Is the lack of scientific respectability of the source enough reason to ignore it completely?

Of the 14,000+ Readings in the Cayce archives, approximately two-thirds deal with health and healing. Specific treatment procedures are outlined for hundreds of conditions. As a personal example: a friend and I developed skin conditions around the same time. He was diagnosed with psoriasis; I with eczema. According to the Readings, both are related to what is now called leaky gut syndrome—a condition perhaps first described in Cayce's work. The recommended treatment was the same for both of us: two kinds of herbal tea and some dietary changes. Within a short time, we were both symptom-free. Modern medical treatment for these conditions often requires months of medications that can be costly and carry serious side effects. Dr. John Pagano has worked for over forty years with the Cayce program. His book, *Healing Psoriasis*, outlines the method and documents remarkable results from those who follow it.

The Master once said, "The works I do you can do—and greater." If so, then perhaps this is a greater work, for it carries forward the same spirit of healing and compassion. Remember, this is not information to be believed so much as it is to be tested and applied. Time and again, those who followed the guidance of the Readings found it to be both accurate and beneficial.

This information is like an unmined vein of gold, its worth exceeding even Fort Knox. One day, it will be rediscovered, and we will witness a great renaissance of wisdom. Perhaps the most significant accomplishment of the Cayce organization has been placing his entire body of work onto a single DVD. This knowledge, like the Bible, belongs to everyone. And as the Readings remind us*: we have only what we give away.*

The Good Shepherd

The essence of the Cayce work is that we—all of humankind and beyond—are "children of the Most High," eternally beloved by our Father. We include and beyond because, on occasion, the Readings refer to the people of the universe. We are not alone.

We were one with Him in the beginning. Yet, like the Prodigal Son, we have all wandered from that unity. As the prophet Isaiah said, "All we like sheep have gone astray; we have turned everyone to his own way." (Isa. 53:6) Now, we are beginning to awaken—to rise and return. Our Father is not willing that *any* of His children should be lost. Like the Good Shepherd who leaves the ninety-nine sheep to seek the one that is missing, He will not rest until all are gathered. Would the One who came to save the world settle for less? Did He create some souls merely as extras? Or are all souls precious?

Clearly, the parable of the Good Shepherd reveals a God of boundless love and forgiveness—one who will not permit a single soul to suffer eternal separation. Cayce affirmed that nothing truer has ever been spoken than that God is not willing that any soul should perish. The sobering reality, however, is that the return to unity may take considerable time—because of our own persistent rebellion. Will we take ages and eons to return? Or will we choose to arise now?

This journey back to Oneness can be greatly shortened if we embrace the way of love demonstrated by Jesus. In His Spirit, and the divine pattern He fulfilled, we find the Way. Consider the past 2,000 years: how much spiritual progress has humanity made? Likely far less than we could have achieved with a true worldview of Oneness. The Readings observe, "The work for the needs of humankind has gone down through thousands and millions of years for hundreds and thousands of years to come."

Even so, we may rejoice—because we now have a pattern and an Advocate, a promise that all of God's children will eventually return home. We, like Jesus, must learn obedience to the Law of Love. Scripture tells us that "He learned obedience through the things He suffered." (Heb. 5:8) Why would even He need to learn obedience? Because He is a soul, just as we are—a brother, a child of God. And He, as Adam, fell.

As we continue to explore a psychology of the soul, we will continue to rely heavily on the material from the Cayce Readings. Citations will include the case number assigned to each seeker. For instance, the first Reading Cayce gave for himself is labeled: 294-1.

Psychics

As with any human endeavor, psychic abilities vary widely in both type and effectiveness. The accuracy and usefulness of the information provided also differ greatly from one psychic to another. Unfortunately, there is widespread misunderstanding about what a good psychic can actually do. Some skeptics quip, "If he's really psychic, why doesn't he win the lottery?"—as if being psychic were the same as being omniscient. This is like asking a world-class violinist to perform a piano concerto and questioning her musicianship when she cannot. A psychic may be deeply gifted and helpful, even if not perfect.

Consider the biblical story of Jonah. God told Jonah that Nineveh would be destroyed. But when the people repented, God changed His mind. This was a prophecy that did not come to pass—demonstrating that spiritual insight may reveal possibilities rather than fixed outcomes. Dismissing the entire field because of frauds or errors is misguided. Every human endeavor—whether politics, medicine, or business—is populated by its share of deceivers and opportunists.

What matters most in psychic work is the intent behind the request. Since God is love, the energy and clarity that flow through us are shaped by our motivations. Love begets love. The desire to help and to offer the most beneficial information enhances the psychic's ability to stay attuned. On the other hand, testing a psychic with trick questions—especially when there is no sincere intention to help someone—can disrupt their attunement. In controlled laboratory settings, when no real-world application is involved, researchers often observe a phenomenon known as the decline effect—where performance diminishes over time. Likewise, psychics who begin with clear insight may lose accuracy if there is no feedback or no meaningful way to help others. Too often, researchers in this field have been more focused on proving the existence of ESP than on understanding its practical use and the laws that govern it.

What's needed is discernment rather than cynicism. In this field, doubt itself interferes with demonstration. I once worked with a twelve-year-old girl who had a remarkable talent. She could read the title of a book's cover and its color simply by running her fingers over it, without ever looking at it. I tested her in a spirit of respect, and her ability was genuine. A well-known researcher, eager to rule out cheating, enclosed her arm in a black box with a cloth sleeve so she could not see the book. The setup was intimidating and foreign to her, and she was unable to perform. The researcher later reported that under "properly controlled conditions," she showed no psychic ability. But in a field like this, proper conditions should be those that help the subject feel at ease—not those designed to provoke failure. A creative researcher can build rigorous controls without sacrificing empathy or respect.

Edgar Cayce himself offered to be studied—if there was someone in genuine need, and if the questions asked were serious and intended to help. Sadly, no one ever took him up on this in a meaningful way.

As Paul wrote in 1 Corinthians 12, "There is one Spirit, but many gifts." Some psychics are simply more gifted than others. Some, like Gerard Croiset, were especially adept at finding lost children. Others specialize in medical diagnosis, past-life readings, energy healing, or communicating with the spirit world. These gifts are often tied to experiences and skills developed in previous lifetimes. *One Spirit, many gifts.*

The most credible psychics—those with a track record of both high accuracy and deep helpfulness—tend to agree on many core spiritual truths. They consistently affirm the existence of God, the divine nature of humanity, the soul's journey through many incarnations, and the unique spiritual authority of Jesus as Master of masters. When several well-regarded psychics independently agree on a topic, and when those agreements prove accurate, we gain a solid basis to trust their insights on other matters. This process mirrors the way scientific truths are established—through replication, validation, and convergence of evidence.

Indeed, numerous scientifically verified events point to the existence and influence of God as the most reasonable explanation. Parapsychology offers us profound insights into the nature of human consciousness—and into a deeper psychology of the soul.

What is psychology, after all? At its core, it is the science of behavior. Psychologists study sensation and perception, physiology, motivation, emotion, learning, heredity, and environment—all in pursuit of understanding how and why we act as we do. One hopes the field will increasingly explore this vast and promising dimension of human potential.

Parapsychology

Parapsychology is a well-established field of scientific inquiry, supported by multiple professional journals that publish rigorously designed and controlled experiments. An extensive body of literature by respected scientists affirms the validity and potential applications of parapsychological phenomena.

There is no reason why the accepted methodologies of science cannot be applied to this field. Nor is there any reason why data derived from parapsychological studies should not be accepted as objective facts—so long as they meet the same standards used in other branches of science. And yet, such data are often dismissed. Why?

The resistance stems largely from dogma, tradition, and vested interests—those who fear what expanded self-understanding might imply. When psychics produce extraordinary results, some self-proclaimed scientists dismiss the findings outright, claiming the outcomes are so improbable they must be fraudulent. Ironically, this rejection is among the most unscientific responses imaginable.

Many of the phenomena studied in parapsychology echo experiences described in the Bible. One might expect students of scripture to welcome scientific evidence that supports the reality of such events. But, paradoxically, much of the Christian community remains skeptical or even openly hostile to this field. Critics argue that human beings, as created creatures, cannot manifest spiritual gifts unless God acts directly through them—and only through devout Christians, in Christian contexts, and with perfect accuracy.

There is a seed of truth in that claim, but a half-truth can often be more misleading than a complete falsehood.

Let's examine some parallels between parapsychological research and biblical stories. The major areas of parapsychological investigation—often referred to as "the big five"—include telepathy, clairvoyance, precognition, psychokinesis, and healing.

Telepathy involves receiving information from another person's mind. When Jesus spoke to the Samaritan woman at the well, she ran to her friends exclaiming, "He told me everything I've ever done."

Clairvoyance is the acquisition of knowledge not present in anyone's mind. For example, when Saul lost his cattle, he sought out the prophet Samuel, who accurately told him where to find them.

Precognition is the ability to perceive future events. Pharaoh's dream of an impending famine was a case of precognition. Joseph's interpretation not only secured his release from prison but also positioned him to save Egypt—and the lineage of the Jewish people. Notably, the dream came to a non-Jewish ruler, showing that divine messages are not limited to religious boundaries.

Psychokinesis is the ability to influence physical objects without physical contact. The prophet Elisha encountered a man distraught over a sunken axe-head. In response, Elisha stirred the water with his staff, and the iron floated to the surface—moved, perhaps, by his compassion and spiritual attunement. Cayce said: it was nothing to make the axe head float, but would you apply that to everything that has sunk? You see, it was the intention that mattered.

Healing, or so-called paranormal healing, appears frequently in scripture, particularly in the life of Jesus. Today, some studies explore the effects of prayer on water used to nourish plants. Water prayed over by a healer has been shown to enhance growth compared to untreated water from the same source. Numerous reputable studies have verified the beneficial effects of prayer on health and healing.

The Bible offers countless examples of such phenomena, and modern research increasingly validates their reality. The Cayce Readings add further depth, offering insights unavailable since "the foundations of the world." Scripture tells us that Jesus taught in parables, "...things which have been kept secret from the foundation of the world" (Matt. 13:35). Paul speaks of a "mystery...which is Christ in you" (Col. 1:26–27). These divine mysteries remain largely unexplored—much like the Readings themselves.

These psychic phenomena follow lawful processes. There are known methods for developing such gifts as expressions of the Spirit. When cultivated and applied wisely, they hold immense potential to benefit humanity. Consider the case of Ambrose Worrall, both an engineer and a healer. During WWII, 26 newly built aircraft were found to be missing two sets of crucial bolts. The planes might have needed to be disassembled—at a time when urgent deployment was critical. Worrall offered to "check them out." Touching each plane, he identified the two in question. His assessment was exactly right, saving time and effort.

This is not "woo-woo nonsense"—it is a practical, concrete application of psychic ability. Ambrose and his wife, Olga Worrall, herself a gifted healer, demonstrated the value of such abilities thousands of times.

There is nothing in this account that should offend religious sensibilities or scientific standards. To dismiss Worrall's discernment as mere luck ignores the extreme improbability of such accuracy. His story is a simple, compelling example of the usefulness of psychic skill—and its vast implications.

Yet we are still told there is "no scientific proof" of ESP. But proof, like beauty, often lies in the eye of the beholder. If one is a dogmatic Christian or an atheistic materialist, any evidence may be preemptively rejected—deemed heretical, fraudulent, or satanic. Instead of addressing *facts*, the conversation devolves into *beliefs*.

Consider a few examples. Actress Jayne Meadows-Allen, in a televised interview, demonstrated the ability to identify which of 52 playing cards had been drawn—accurately and without trickery. The person she amazed immediately asked, "Do you believe in ESP?"—shifting the focus from direct evidence to personal belief, as if that somehow invalidated the demonstration.

On a trip to Mexico, I encountered a British physicist who had apparently disparaged our group's interest in ESP. When we met, I asked if he had read any peer-reviewed studies in this field. His response was telling: "I don't have to. I already know there's nothing to it!" His worldview had closed the door to honest inquiry—the very foundation of scientific method.

Let it be stated clearly: any scientist who categorically denies the findings of parapsychology does so not on scientific grounds, but for philosophical or emotional reasons.

Scientists with Half-Closed Minds

Even some of the most esteemed parapsychologists of the late twentieth century maintained closed minds about key facts—especially those touching on the religious or spiritual dimensions of psychic phenomena. A striking example of this is the widespread disinterest in the profoundly rich and meaningful work of Edgar Cayce. I share the following stories not as criticisms of these accomplished individuals, but rather to illustrate how cultural biases can prevent even great minds from giving this material the serious examination it deserves.

Consider J.B. Rhine, a pioneer in parapsychology who conducted influential research at Duke University and published widely. When I asked him about Cayce, he replied that he had looked into it and found "nothing there." Later, I learned that Rhine had once sought a Cayce Reading for his daughter, who had a health issue. The Reading included a diagnosis, a treatment protocol, and a recommendation to use a device called the radio-active appliance—a healing instrument developed from the Source of the Readings and priced at twenty-five dollars. Rhine was apparently so offended by the price and the suggestion of such a device that he dismissed the entire Cayce methodology as fraudulent. Ironically, the diagnosis had been accurate, but the treatment was never pursued.

Next, consider Gardner Murphy, an outstanding psychologist and author of books across multiple areas of psychology, including *The Challenge of Psychical Research.* When I asked his opinion of Cayce, he responded, "Oh, we looked into that. There was nothing there." What he didn't realize was that the Cayce organization had preserved copies of every piece of correspondence they ever received. Murphy's "investigation" had been limited to a single case. He had asked a physician from Columbia University to review a Cayce Reading. The doctor dismissed the Reading as "gobbledy-gook," and Murphy accepted that verdict as definitive—an astonishingly shallow approach for someone dedicated to scientific inquiry.

A third example is Dr. Ian Stevenson, a widely respected psychiatrist who later became known for his rigorous research on reincarnation at the University of Virginia. Before embarking on that work, Stevenson published an insightful article in *The Atlantic* titled *Scientists with Half-Closed Minds.*

At the request of Hugh Lynn Cayce, I presented Stevenson with several Cayce Readings that included past-life information—specifically, recommendations for present-life occupations based on past experiences. As soon as Stevenson read a reference to the time of a well-known individual named Richelieu in one Reading, he dismissed it, claiming the date was historically inaccurate. He did not read further. Had he continued, he would have seen that the Reading clarified that the Richelieu in question was *not* the famous cardinal but another historical figure. Yet, that brief glance was the end of our meeting.

In all three cases, these distinguished scholars—whom I continue to respect—rejected one of the richest sources of psychic insight available based on superficial or emotionally charged reasons. Stevenson, in particular, rejected what could have been groundbreaking material on reincarnation due to a single misunderstood historical detail. This same lack of thorough examination is true of several other prominent researchers who have endorsed far less gifted psychics than Cayce.

One possible reason for this pattern of rejection is that the Cayce Readings affirm the story of Jesus—not merely as myth or metaphor but as a cosmic and spiritual reality. The religious dimensions of Cayce's worldview may be too challenging for those committed to either a rigidly scientific or strictly doctrinal framework. It becomes easy to dismiss the Cayce legacy as a "cult" or to ignore it altogether when a full engagement would require a complete paradigm shift.

Such resistance is not uncommon in the face of dramatically new information. As Stevenson himself observed, many scientists today are working with "half-closed minds."

I recall speaking with a young man about Cayce who said, "He couldn't have been very important; I've never heard of him." And that raises a fair question: *If Cayce's work is so profound, why is it not more widely known?* I share stories like these not only to highlight the dismissive tendencies of even well-meaning researchers, but also to underscore a deeper cultural reluctance to grapple with the vast worldview implications of Cayce's work.

We all—parapsychologists included—still carry one foot in the old worldview. The Cayce Readings present a profound challenge to both Christian theology and conventional scientific thinking. When one's career, credibility, or worldview is on the line, it is understandable—though regrettable—that some may hesitate to move forward.

Psychical Research

Psychical research, while closely related to the more formally scientific discipline of parapsychology, has found perhaps greater development and emphasis in England than in the United States. In the British context, this research has often centered on mediumship—the communication with individuals in the spirit plane—and the question of the soul's survival after physical death. Studies in this area have employed rigorous and sophisticated research designs, enabling researchers to claim a high degree of accuracy and credibility in their findings. Many of these investigations have sought specifically to demonstrate the continued existence of consciousness following bodily death.

A clear distinction must be made between *spiritualism*, especially as it is commonly practiced in England, and *spirituality* as an inner, transformative orientation. British spiritualists often encourage mediums to work with a specific spirit guide from the other side, emphasizing this as a safeguard for authentic communication. This practice, however, has made many British spiritualists less open to the idea of reincarnation, as their framework focuses more on linear continuity in the afterlife than on cyclical rebirth. Some spiritualists have even criticized Edgar Cayce because he did not rely on a spirit guide. Cayce, however, was instructed by his Source to seek guidance only through the Master, Jesus. As the Readings asked, "Why turn to any other when He is so high?"

Today we are fortunate to have examples like Edgar Cayce—psychics whose records of accuracy and helpfulness are difficult to dispute. We also have a scientifically grounded field of parapsychology that validates the reality of psychic abilities through rigorous experimentation. Additionally, the broader domain of psychical research, extending over more than a century, has produced a remarkable body of evidence documenting a wide range of psychic phenomena. Beyond these academic and institutional sources, we have countless compelling reports of personal experiences that attest to the same truths.

And yet, despite this abundance of data and testimony, many Christian churches and members of the scientific community still refuse even to consider the facts. Perhaps, as Carl Jung suggested, this resistance stems from a deep and primal fear—a "panic fear"—of what the study of the unconscious mind might uncover. But Jung also pointed out that when we confront the darker aspects of ourselves and bring them into conscious integration, these once-frightening forces can become powerful allies rather than dangerous masters.

Carl Jung, unquestionably one of the greatest psychologists of the twentieth century, addressed this very point in his profound essay *The Undiscovered Self*. There, he asserted unequivocally:

"We can no longer practice any psychology that denies the facts of parapsychology."

CHAPTER 3
MODELS AND THEORIES

SCIENTISTS AND SYSTEMATIC thinkers often use models as frameworks or illustrations to help clarify the components of their theories. The purposes of a model are: to organize what we already know, help us discover new relationships, and prevent us from being overwhelmed by the full complexity of a subject. A model is not meant to represent reality itself, but to serve as a tool for systematic thought. An effective model can be applied in a variety of contexts. When new facts raise further questions, a model may assist in revealing new insights. For these reasons, I will refer to models throughout this book to aid in deepening our understanding.

Here are some illustrations of models and examples of how they may be used. Careful study of the diagrams that follow in this book will assist the reader in understanding the text.

In one of Freud's models, he proposed that the mind is like an iceberg—only one-eighth (the conscious) above the surface, and seven-eighths (the unconscious) submerged. Jung believed that Freud's concept of the unconscious covered only a neurotic layer and that beneath it lay a much deeper and more expansive level, which he called the "collective unconscious." According to Jung, this deeper unconscious contains a number of archetypal patterns shared by all human beings. Since Jung also accepted the validity of parapsychological phenomena, we may invert and open his model at the top—reimagining it as a *funnel.* An open top suggests our full access to the powers and knowledge of the Spirit. The funnel becomes a fitting model for the frequently repeated concept in the Readings that the Infinite finds expression in our lives as the Finite: from the Infinite into the Finite.

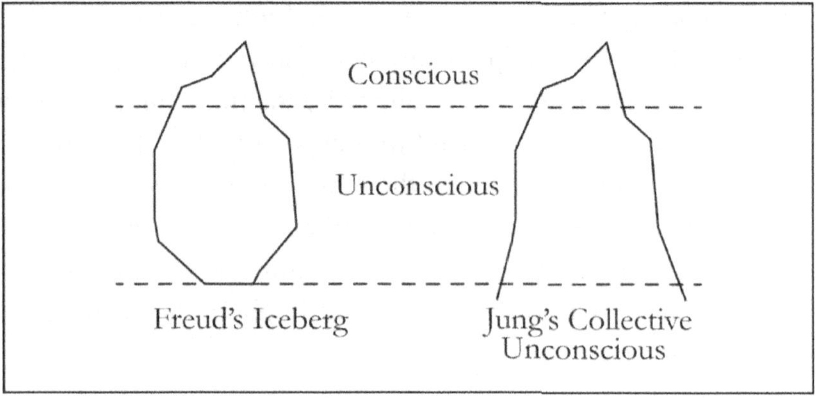

Figure 3: Freud / Jung Comparison

The Readings strongly encourage us to study the power of the subconscious:

> "The knowledge of the subconscious of an entity, or an individual, in or of the human family, is of one force, or element, or self in the creation of the human family, and until the entity, or individual, as individuals, make this known to

> groups, classes, countries, nations, THE GREATER STUDY OF SELF, that force will only be magnified."
> (3744-5 p2)

This may mean, as Jung warned, that unless we gain a deeper understanding of the unconscious, dark forces may arise from it and become increasingly problematic for humanity. Considering the vast number of social and political challenges, this certainly appears to be the case in our present time.

The funnel concept is used here as a model derived from one of Edgar Cayce's dreams. Cayce described seeing a "cone," "trumpet," or "funnel," and said that this imagery would help deepen our understanding. The funnel, wide at the top and narrow at the bottom, is an excellent image for representing the soul's purpose. We were created to be co-creators with the Father—channels through which spiritual energy can be expressed creatively. We have access to the Infinite energies of the universe, and we are gifted with the ability to manifest those energies in finite, creative acts. The funnel symbolizes this purpose, especially for the soul incarnate on Earth. It graphically illustrates our role as conduits for God's love. The full attunement of the soul to the Infinite is demonstrated in the life of Jesus. This is who we were at the beginning; this is who we are meant to become in full realization.

Another valuable model was developed by Carl Jung. He described the Self as the center of our being and drew a line through it, indicating that part is conscious and part unconscious. What Jung called the Self corresponds with what

I refer to as the Soul. In his model, the ego is situated above the Self, and the Persona above the ego. Below the Self are the Shadow and the Animus/Anima. The goal of individuation is to move consciousness into the Self. The more consciousness shifts toward the ego or Persona, the more the unconscious contents—Shadow and Animus/Anima — are repressed and become problematic. This aligns with the model I will develop: when the lower centers seek to dominate instead of yield, the individual becomes ruled by the lower forces.

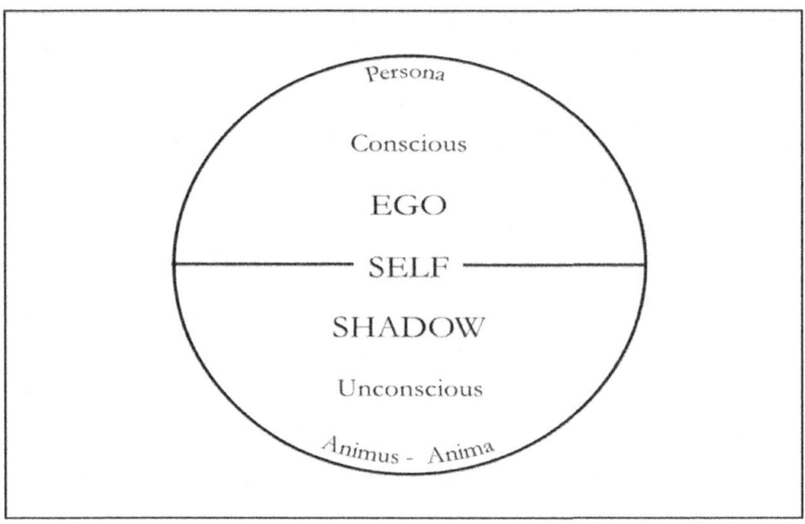

Figure 4: Jung's Model of Self

As souls, we are manifestations of the Infinite into the Finite. This is the fully attuned consciousness of Jesus and our own destiny. We are presently cut off in consciousness due to our cumulative choices.

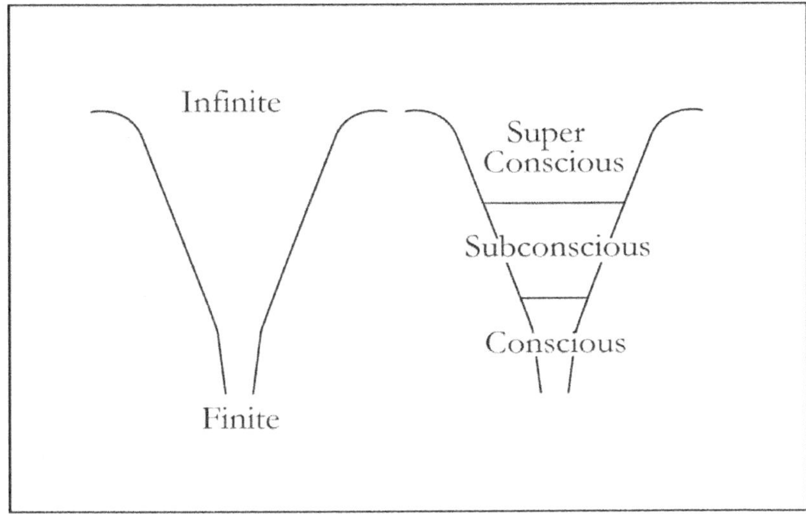

Figure 5: Infinite Manifesting in The Finite

Using this model, aligns with our understanding of three-dimensional experience.

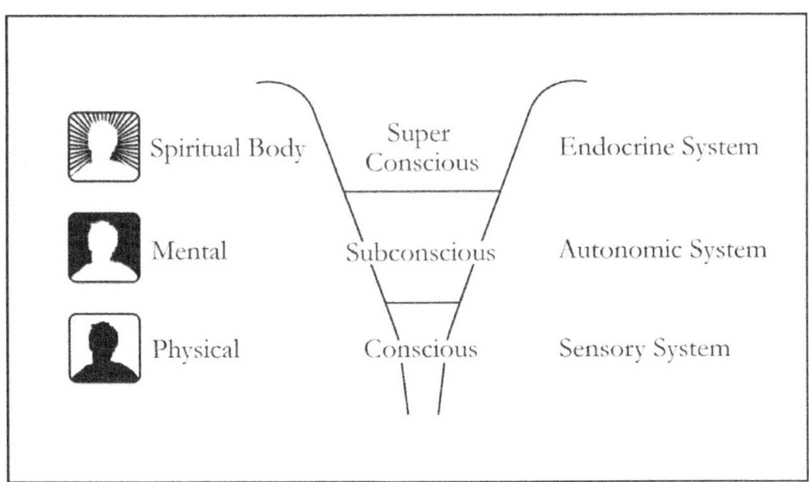

Figure 6: Correlation of Consciousness and the Physical

We have three bodies: the spiritual body (the soul), the mental body, and the physical body (Figure 6). We also have three levels of consciousness: the superconscious potential, the subconscious, and the conscious. And we have three physiological systems that correspond to these: the endocrine system, the autonomic nervous system, and the sensory system. Jung emphasized that the more we identify with the superficial Persona, the more vulnerable we become to the unconscious Shadow and Animus/Anima. In our terms, this dynamic is represented by the lower centers trying to override the proper leadership of the higher spiritual centers. In Revelation, it is said that the four beasts must bow down.

When we direct the Life Force into expressions not in harmony with the Law of Love, we create barriers to its flow. By disconnecting from the higher consciousness of the soul and limiting ourselves to three-dimensional awareness, we rely solely on the five senses. Yet even in this limited state, we retain access to the subconscious records of the soul, as well as the potential to experience the superconscious or Universal Consciousness—the fullness of divine awareness. This is the level from which the Cayce Readings were accessed.

These levels of consciousness correspond exactly with the pattern of the Old Testament tabernacle. When we attune to the Holy of Holies within ourselves we, like the ancient priests, may meet God face-to-face.

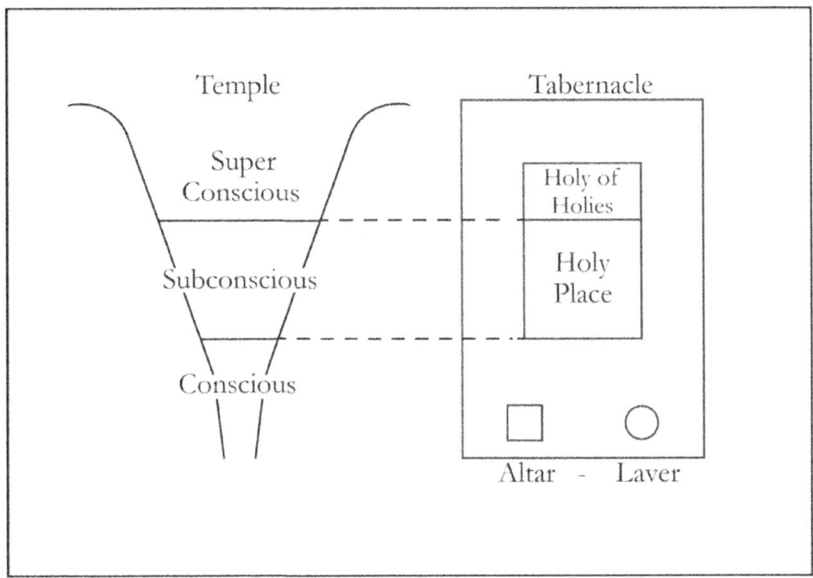

Figure 7: The Tabernacle Pattern of Consciousness Levels

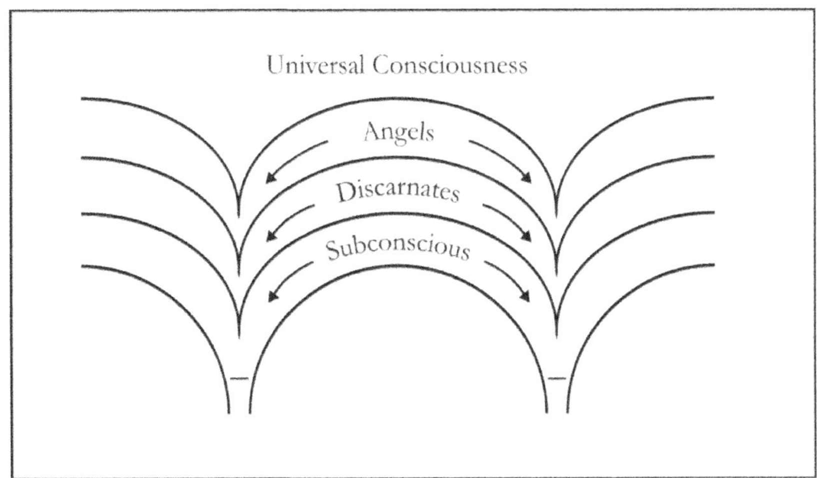

Figure 8: Telepathy, Prayer and Spirit Plane Communication

All subconscious minds are potentially interconnected.

Figure 8 shows how one person's thoughts may influence—or be received by—another through telepathy. Different levels of consciousness and thought vibrate at different frequencies. The Readings teach that "thoughts are things." These vibrations may be compared to the non-material waves used in radio and television where different stations are accessible on their own frequencies or channels. In much the same way, the prayers of one person may powerfully affect the subconscious mind and even the body of another.

We may also be influenced by, or become aware of, other incarnate souls, disincarnate souls, beings from other dimensions, angelic forces, and ascended masters. All subconscious minds are potentially in touch with all others at the several levels of awareness.

Because our subconscious contains records of past lives, we can see how a karmic pattern may be activated in the present. An experience from a past life, when triggered, can manifest as karma. Yet if the pattern is awakened and redirected for spiritual growth, the result may look entirely different. Two alcoholics may share the same karmic root. For one, it leads to personal decline. For the other, who chooses a spiritual path—perhaps by becoming an AA sponsor—the same pattern becomes a means of service to others.

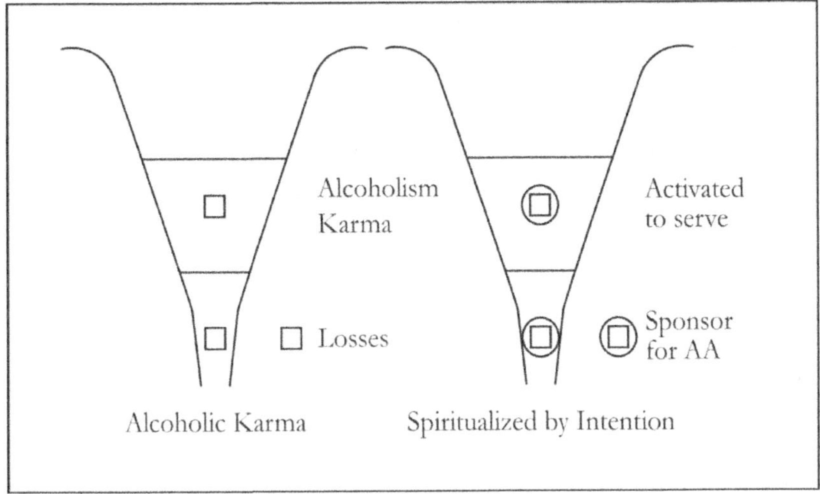

Figure 9: Karmic Manifestations Depend Upon Intent

Within each of us is also a pattern of the Christ. If we choose to activate this pattern, the Readings affirm: "He is thy karma, if you put your trust wholly in Him."

These examples show how models may aid our understanding of a wide range of experiences. Seekers may use these models to gain deeper insights into the phenomena of their own lives.

The mind is the builder: it shapes how the Spirit expresses itself. God is love. The Spirit is love. And the Spirit seeks to flow through patterns of love. The quality of this expression depends on our purposes, intentions, desires, and ideals—these are the essence of the spiritual. When our intentions align with the Law of Love, health and positive impact follow. When our purposes are self-centered, the flow of love is blocked, resulting in confusion, disorder, or even illness.

The soul fulfills God's purpose only by *intending* to manifest selfless love. Thus, we are commanded to love God—and that includes loving His ways of Being, often called Universal Laws. One of the simplest of these laws is: like begets like. If we are unkind to others, we invite unkindness upon ourselves. This is not divine punishment; rather, it reflects the vibrational pattern we have chosen. We draw to ourselves experiences that match our energetic state.

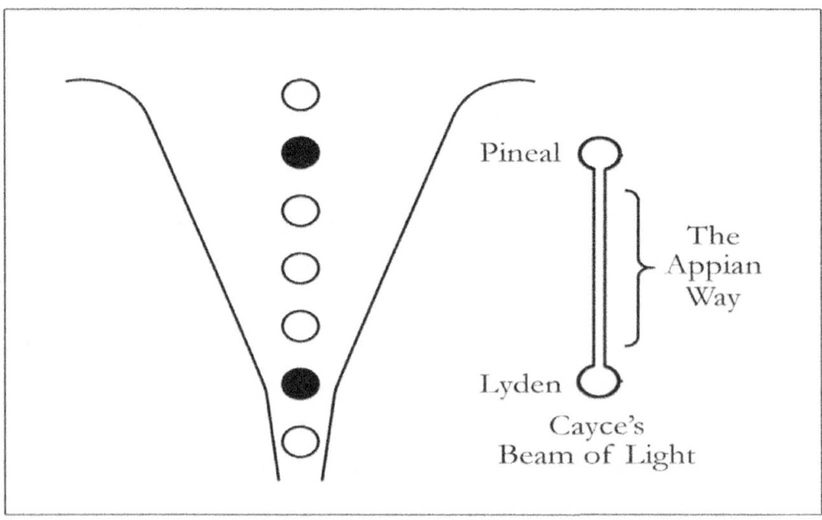

Figure 10: Cayce Felt Like a Dot Rising On a Beam of Light

Another model from the Readings describes the seven spiritual centers of the soul, which correspond to the seven endocrine glands in the body. The spiritual centers reside in the soul. Their physical counterparts are found in the endocrine system. These three bodies—spiritual, mental, and physical—are unified in the incarnate human being.

Edgar Cayce described his inward experience as he prepared to give a Reading. He felt like a dot following a beam of light. As he ascended, he became aware of shadows and movements and knew not to be distracted by them. As he continued upward, the surroundings grew brighter. Eventually, he reached the "hall of records." Later, he understood that this was a meditative state. The beam of light represented the path from the Lyden to the Pineal—the "open door"—and then to the Pituitary. When activated, the Pituitary gave him access to Universal Consciousness. We will explore this further in the following pages.

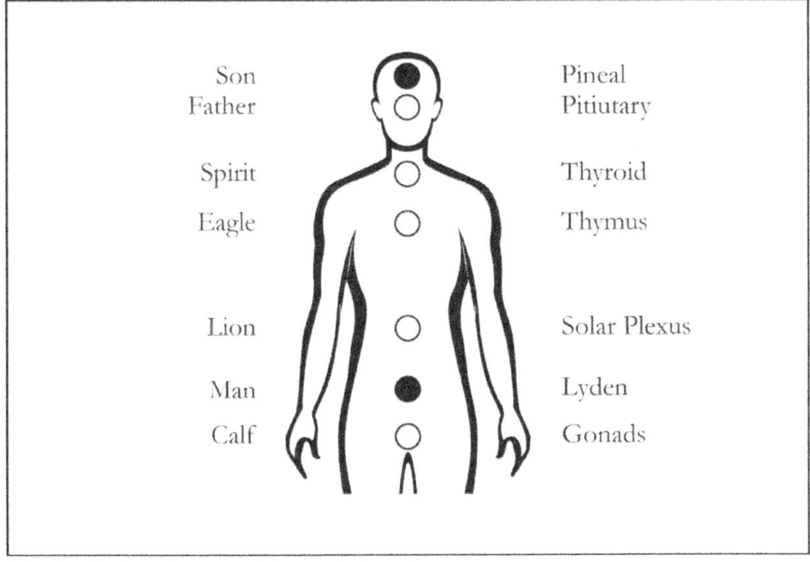

Figure 11: Spiritual and Physical Correlates

The spiritual centers are in the spiritual body – the soul. The physiological correlates of these centers are the endocrine glands. The four lower centers are seen in John's Revelation as a calf, man, lion and eagle. The link between the spiritual and physical bodies is mediated by the mental body. The mental body's physiological correlate—the subconscious—is the autonomic nervous system, which includes the sympathetic and parasympathetic branches. The Pineal and Lyden are associated with the parasympathetic system, which connects at both the top (cranial) and bottom (sacral) of the spinal cord. The sympathetic system governs daily activity; the parasympathetic governs rest, healing, and the creative aspects of sexuality.

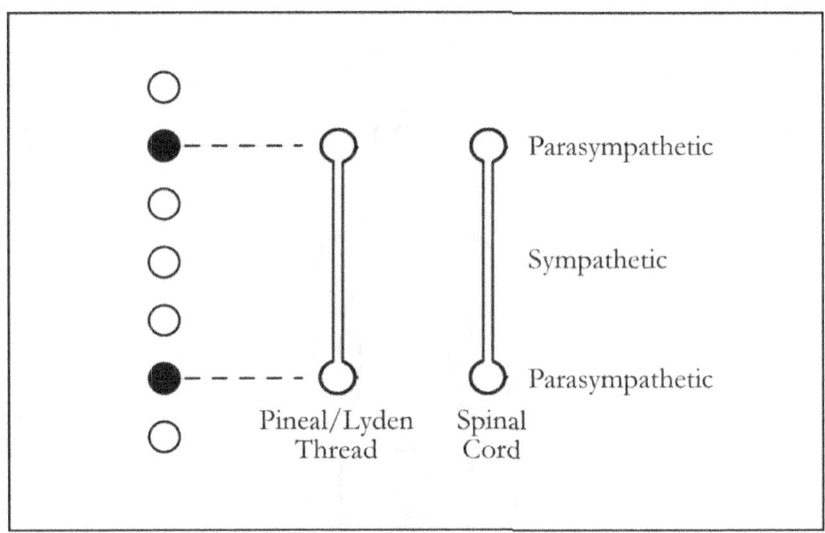

Figure 12: The Centers and the Autonomic Nervous System

In deep meditation, parasympathetic dominance must be established—similar to the conditions required in deep hypnosis. Herbert Benson's *The Relaxation Response* describes the physiological shift from sympathetic to parasympathetic dominance as central to the meditative process.

In *The Law of Psychic Phenomena*, a book highly recommended by the Readings, Thomas Hudson uses the terms "objective" and "subjective" minds. Hypnosis involves a shift from the dominance of the objective mind to the subjective mind—a state in which psychic phenomena become more likely. This state is also marked by parasympathetic dominance and involves stimulation of the Lyden and Pineal. Achieving this state is one of the goals of meditation.

Preparation for meditation closely resembles preparation for hypnosis. Students of meditation can benefit from learning hypnotic induction techniques, especially self-hypnosis, which may include progressive relaxation, regulated breathing, counting, and visualization. It is important to remember that Cayce cautioned against meditating when not in a good physical condition. If one's symptoms are such that attunement is not felt, we should avoid meditating.

> Q-6: Should one meditate when not in a good physical condition?
>
> A-6: As we have given on prayer and meditation, when one can separate self sufficiently to be able to meditate properly it is helpful. When one cannot, best not to attempt it.
> (281-18)

The funnel model illustrates that our access to Spirit—our awareness of God—must move through our inner systems. The

Spirit must pass through the endocrine system, then the parasympathetic system, and then, as the Revelation teaches, there must be a "bowing down" of the sensory system and the four lower centers. All of these steps are necessary for deep meditation. The sensory system must surrender its demand for attention. The lower centers must yield their claim to dominance. For instance, if anger occupies our awareness, the lion—the solar plexus center—takes over. Everything we may know of God must pass through these systems. These conditions may arise spontaneously during a moment of joy, a beautiful sunset, the smile of a child, or a genuine desire to help someone.

We all know the scripture: "The Lord was not in the wind, nor in the earthquake, nor in the fire, but in a still small voice." (1 Kings 19:11–12) The implication is that our prayers must be offered in quietness.

The Readings equate the imaginative forces with the kundalini forces. These same forces are the basis of the profound experiences found in hypnosis and meditation. There is a long history of research connecting hypnosis with psychic development—including the story of Edgar Cayce. The first line in *There Is a River*—a Cayce biography—reads: "The story of Edgar Cayce properly belongs in the history of hypnosis."

CHAPTER 4
STATES OF CONSCIOUSNESS

WE HAVE DEFINED God as being virtually synonymous with Universal Consciousness. This is the state of attunement from which the Edgar Cayce Readings were delivered. All souls—god-beings made in His image—possess the same infinite potential for such consciousness. The Readings affirm that we experience many dimensions of consciousness. As the Master said, "In my Father's house are many mansions." According to the Readings, we are currently sojourning within a solar system that represents eight dimensions, though our earthly experience is mostly limited to three-dimensional awareness.

Even so, while incarnate on Earth, the soul may have experiences in other dimensions. However, these experiences can only be brought into conscious awareness through three-dimensional interpretation. For example, the Readings explain that during sleep the soul may visit another dimension, yet upon waking, the experience is remembered as a dream—an interpretive translation into the language of three-dimensional consciousness.

All physical states of consciousness are accompanied by complex and profound biochemical processes. We are aware that substances such as alcohol, psychoactive drugs like LSD, anesthetics, and others can alter, intensify, or expand consciousness. In human biochemistry, the "lock and key" model applies: for an externally administered substance to affect consciousness, a corresponding receptor site must exist within the body. If such a receptor exists, it implies that the body has the potential to produce a similar chemical internally.

Athletes often describe a "runner's high," a euphoric state caused by the body's production of endogenous opioids. Likewise, the body generates distinct chemistries associated with anger, sexual arousal, and, more rarely, elevated spiritual states. Every substance we ingest has the potential to influence consciousness. One surprising Reading (274-10) claims that people who consume large quantities of hot peppers tend toward vengeance. If this is true, the implications for the influence of other substances—even common foods—are significant. The psychoactive compounds needed for heightened states of consciousness are created within the endocrine system itself.

As previously discussed, we exist in three dimensions with three distinct but unified bodies: the spiritual body (the soul), the mental body, and the physical body. While these are one in essence, they may function independently, as demonstrated by out-of-body experiences. Thus, unity among the three is not necessarily spatial but vibrational. The ideal condition is attunement—when body and mind are aligned with spirit. Both healing and meditation aim to achieve this attunement, which is always the spiritual goal.

Whether incarnate or discarnate, in or out of the body, the soul's range of conscious experience is virtually limitless.

The Readings describe many states of consciousness, using terms such as:

- God's other door
- the interims
- the inter-between
- the material
- the borderland
- the shadow
- just passed over
- the unseen forces
- outer darkness
- the world of unconsciousness
- the infinite
- the Throne of Grace/before the throne
- the Glory

These expressions may overlap in meaning, but they offer insight into the multidimensional nature of consciousness as described in the Readings.

What is meant by "outer darkness"? In *Return from Tomorrow*, Dr. George Ritchie recounts a near-death experience from his youth. Out of his body, he is guided by Jesus through several realms. In one, he observes souls completely alone in darkness, seemingly abandoned. Later, passing through that same realm again, he perceives spirit beings working to awaken these souls to the possibility of moving toward the light.

In *Testimony of Light*, Helen Greaves, while still incarnate, receives telepathic communication from her friend Frances Banks, now in the spirit plane. A former Anglican nun, Frances describes her work helping "lost souls." On one occasion, she shares that she and others have received a difficult assignment: to assist the soul of a former high-ranking German officer under Hitler. This soul, blind and covered in what he believed were sores—symbolic of his guilt—had dwelt in darkness for years. With him came the soul of a young Jewish mother, attached to him by hatred, holding him responsible for the deaths of her husband and child. Frances notes that the woman would be the easier to help of the two. Spirit plane helpers have greater difficulty helping a self-condemning soul. If our anger or guilt is turned inward we will be less able to receive assistance in the spirit plane. This powerful story underscores a spiritual law: if hatred is not replaced by forgiveness, the hater remains locked in vibrational alignment with the one they despise.

Such accounts are sobering and suggest "outer darkness" is a self-created state, a result of self-condemnation and internalized guilt. Are we placed in darkness by external forces? It appears true that our hatred links us to others through shared vibrational resonance—even beyond death. The Readings warn that what we habitually dwell upon in the physical realm becomes what manifests and possesses us in the spirit realm.

These examples serve as urgent reminders: **mind is the builder**, and states of consciousness are shaped by our own choices. Therefore, we must discipline our thoughts toward the positive and be willing to forgive—even those who have knowingly harmed us. If we continue to harbor hatred, we remain tied to the object of our resentment. The Readings repeatedly affirm that all subconscious minds are potentially connected. In hypnosis, the connection between hypnotist and subject is known as rapport. This rapport may include telepathic contact. On a visit to Russian parapsychologists, my group learned of a case in which a hypnotized subject could be re-hypnotized telepathically from several miles away.

Because all subconscious minds are interconnected, we may be vulnerable to the negative or manipulative thoughts of others. Thus, we must be vigilant in praying for protection—for ourselves and for others. Such prayers are especially recommended at bedtime.

We are currently within a solar system comprised of eight dimensions. Between lifetimes, or during a lifetime in the dream state, we may sojourn in any or all of these dimensions and even beyond. The range of consciousness available to us is vaster than we can presently comprehend in three dimensions.

Experiencing Elevated Consciousness

The human body has seven spiritual centers, akin to inner senses. Each center supports a different level of awareness. We may be thought of as seven-story buildings—some with elevators that stop at only one floor. Some psychics, though gifted, may attune to only one specific level. What they perceive there may be accurate, but it remains partial. Some good sensitives even deny reincarnation because their awareness is limited to the dimension in which they are attuned.

Higher states of consciousness may be nurtured through a variety of means: altered breathing, meditation, music, sound, hypnosis, chanting, incense, stones and gems, our reading material, and—most importantly—how we speak and behave in our relationships. Elevated states of awareness, including experiences of white light and even Cosmic Consciousness, are attainable while still incarnate, as demonstrated by the research of Robert Monroe.

Monroe successfully facilitated enhanced states of consciousness through the use of layered sound frequencies. A recording engineer by profession, he became deeply interested in consciousness expansion following a series of spontaneous out-of-body experiences. After confirming through medical evaluation that he had no physical or psychological disorders, Monroe pursued a series of experiments into higher states of awareness, driven by personal curiosity and intellectual rigor. His strong interest in the impact of sound on human consciousness—particularly its role in improving learning and inducing relaxation—led him to systematically explore, understand, and eventually replicate altered states of awareness. His work enabled individuals to access such states as deep relaxation, lucid dreaming, and out-of-body experiences.

Through his explorations, Monroe charted a spectrum of consciousness states, ranging from ordinary waking awareness to encounters with non-physical energies and intelligences—often described as guides or beings of higher evolution, echoing the accounts found in the Cayce readings.

Cayce described the state from which he delivered Readings as a Universal Consciousness. This level of attunement is available to all. One Reading encourages us:

> Be satisfied with nothing short of a Universal Consciousness, guided or guarded by the Lord of the Way, or the Way itself. In Him is Life. Why be satisfied with a lesser portion than a whole measure? (Reading 281, p. 189)

How can we attain this Universal Consciousness? It may seem unreachable when we consider Cayce's extraordinary abilities. Yet the Readings provide simple and practical guidance. We are told that no one has strayed so far that they cannot turn inward and receive divine guidance—even on seemingly trivial matters. When faced with decisions, whether major or minor, the following process is recommended:

- Set an ideal or intention against which to measure the decision.
- Frame your question so it can be answered with a *yes* or *no*.
- Consciously decide: *Yes, I am going to do this.*
- Compare this decision with your ideal. *Is it aligned with my values?*

- Meditate—not on the question itself, but to achieve attunement.
- Say, *Lord, I have decided to do this. Shall I?* Listen.
- Be receptive: you may hear an inner voice or receive a feeling. Capture that feeling.
- Reassess the decision against your ideal.
- If you receive confirmation, act and express gratitude.

The question may be repeated at different times, in different levels of attunement. Practice with low-risk decisions to learn how this process works for you. Often, you will receive an additional insight or message. Continue to refine your approach. A fuller explanation of this technique is found in *The Edgar Cayce Primer*.

When seekers asked for deep or complex information, Cayce's Source insisted they pose questions as yes/no. This prevented confusion from receiving too much information at once. We are urged to act on what we already know, and the next step will be given. According to the Readings, any question is appropriate—whether it concerns finding fishing worms or performing a concerto. The Universal Law still applies: **Seek and you will find. Ask, and it shall be given.**

Sleep and dreams are vital to understanding the activities of the soul. The Readings on these topics are so extensive and profound, they warrant a companion book on this study: *Dreams: The Light of the Night.*

These many paths to higher states of awareness are divine gifts to the soul. When we fixate solely on our waking, three-dimensional consciousness and label it "the real world," we deny ourselves the vast richness of awareness that is our rightful inheritance.

CHAPTER 5
THE ARCHETYPAL BIBLE

"The essential content of all *mythologies* and all *religions* and all *isms* is archetypal."
Carl Jung

For many people today, the Bible may seem passé. The authority claimed by science and the serious theological difficulties within Christianity have led many to dismiss this remarkable book entirely. Yet even now, as noted, the Bible arguably remains the most influential book in the world. The real issue is not whether one must "believe in" it, but rather whether it contains anything worthy of reflection and action. The answer, if approached with a spirit of inquiry, is still yes.

Although there is a long-standing recognition that the Bible is rich in symbolism, there is little agreement—and often little insight—into the meaning or function of its symbols. Even less common is the awareness of any practical or life-enhancing applications arising from these symbolic insights. If we neglect to explore the deeper layers of these symbols, we may overlook the central purpose of the Bible itself. Martin Luther, by insisting that the Bible contained only exoteric and not esoteric meanings, did a significant disservice to later Christian understanding.

While its symbols may initially appear obscure, much like dreams, the Bible itself offers guidance on how to interpret them. The most meaningful of these symbols can be described as archetypal—a concept closely associated with Carl Jung, the Swiss psychologist. Although definitions of archetypes can be confusing, we find a compelling one within the Bible itself. The Old Testament's design and function of the tabernacle, and the New Testament's insight that the body is the temple, both point to the key word: "pattern." This word appears explicitly in both Exodus (OT) and Hebrews (NT). The "pattern" represents the archetypal structure and process within each of us that can lead to an awareness of the Divine and ultimately, to a face-to-face encounter with God.

This term "pattern" is emphasized with great force in both Testaments. Jungian analyst Edward Edinger, in his profound work *Archetype of the Apocalypse*, states, "…an archetype is a pattern." The Old Testament tabernacle and its rituals symbolize internal structures and processes—archetypes—that reside within the human body, the temple of the seeker. Therefore, the outward worship of the Old Testament may be reinterpreted as inward instructions for the modern meditator seeking divine attunement. Remember: an archetype is a pattern.

Exodus 25:8–9 commands, “Let them make me a sanctuary; that I may dwell among them. According to all that I shew thee, after the pattern of the tabernacle, and the pattern of all the tabernacle instruments thereof, even so shall you make it.” And Exodus 25:40 reinforces this: “Look that thou make them after the pattern, which was shewed thee in the mount.” Consider also Deut. 30:11–14, Jer. 31:33–34, and Heb. 8:10–11:

> I will put my laws into their mind, and write them in their hearts...

Deuteronomy 30:11–14 explains:

> This commandment...is not hidden from thee, neither is it far off... But the word is very nigh unto thee, in thy mouth, and in thy heart, that thou mayest do it.

In Romans 10:5–8, Paul offers an interpretation:

> Say not in thine heart, Who shall ascend into heaven? (that is, to bring Christ down) ... But what saith it? The word is nigh thee, even in thy heart: that is, the word of faith, which we preach.

This passage makes clear that the divine law written within us is the Christ within—the archetypal pattern through which we may come to know Him. The Word in our hearts is the Logos of John 1. It is “the mystery...now made manifest...which is Christ in you,” as affirmed in Col. 1:27.

Aspects of this pattern may be activated pathologically. Periodically we hear of a psychiatric patient who feels he is and claims to be Jesus. *The Three Christs of Ypsilanti* gives accounts of three patients in a psychiatric hospital who all claimed to be Jesus. When people claim to be Jesus, they are triggering that pattern which enables all of us to become Christ-like.

In Hebrews, the role of the Old Testament priests is discussed. The high priest would enter the Holy of Holies once a year to meet the Lord face-to-face. These priests, we are told,

> ...serve unto the example and shadow of heavenly things... See, saith he, that thou make all things according to the pattern shewed thee in the mount. (Heb 8:5)

Jeremiah affirms the new covenant:

> I will put my law in their inward parts, and write it in their hearts... they shall all know me, from the least of them to the greatest of them. (Jer. 31:33–34)

These passages detail how the tabernacle's form and functions mirror inner realities. Hebrews 9:23–24 explains:

> It was necessary that the patterns of things in the heavens should be purified... but the heavenly things themselves with better sacrifices than these. For Christ is not entered into the holy places made with hands... but into heaven itself.

This suggests that the physical tabernacle was a symbolic, material representation of a higher, inward reality—an external enactment of an internal process.

Hebrews 10:4–7 continues:

> For it is not possible that the blood of bulls and of goats should take away sins... Sacrifice and offering thou wouldst not, but a body hast thou prepared for me... to do thy will, O God.

Psalm 40 and Hebrews 10:10 clarify: Jesus was prepared not as a sin offering, but as one who would live out the will of God. His prayer in Gethsemane, "not my will but thine, O Lord," reveals His total obedience. His sanctification became ours "by a new and living way." His body was not offered to appease divine wrath, but to live out perfect love. In this, He revealed the pattern of what we are meant to become.

Hebrews 2:11 (NRSV) tells us: "He that sanctifieth and they who are sanctified are all of one origin: for which cause he is not ashamed to call them brethren." As Jesus' spiritual siblings, we are of the same kind and purpose.

The Old Testament tabernacle was an archetypal pattern later fulfilled in the human body as temple. Jesus embodied and demonstrated that pattern, offering us a path to walk.

It's important to remember that the Passover lamb of the Exodus was not a sin offering. It was a symbol of protection and sustenance for the journey. So too, in the Lord's Supper, the elements symbolize nourishment for a spiritual journey, not a payment for sin.

This raises the most difficult theological question: Did God truly require the sacrifice of His Son for the sins of His children? Couldn't a loving God simply forgive? The four pillars of traditional Christian theology—creation ex nihilo, incarnation, Trinity, and vicarious atonement—are not at all Biblical. The idea of vicarious atonement, in particular, is highly problematic.

That theology goes: Human sin was so great that only a terrible, compensatory sacrifice could satisfy God's justice. So His Son volunteered to suffer and die in our place. This proposition led Teilhard de Chardin, in *The Heart of Matter*, to call such theology "artificial and infantile." He was right.

Scripture repeatedly affirms that God takes no pleasure in sacrifice. Why then would He take pleasure in His Son's agony? The real sacrifice required of us all is self-will. Jesus came "to do thy will," learning obedience (Heb. 5:8), and in doing so, manifested the law of love written within the soul—the Christ pattern. This pattern now resides within us all. The primary sin is rebellion; the solution is obedience to love.

When Jesus died, the veil of the temple was torn—signifying a new access for all to the Holy of Holies within ourselves.

Yet Hebrews 9:19–23 contains a curious assertion: "Without shedding of blood is no remission." Examining this symbolically, not literally, reveals the deeper truth.

The rituals of blood sprinkling had no intrinsic efficacy. But symbolically, they point toward internal purification.

Remember: the hormones of the endocrine glands enter directly into the bloodstream. The Pineal gland represents the Christ center. In deep meditation, when the energies rise from the Lyden, through the gonads and upward through the centers to the Pineal, an elixir is secreted. The Leydig cells, located near the gonads, contribute to this. The Pineal activation overflows into the bloodstream—"my cup runneth over." This purified blood revitalizes the 144,000 perfect cells—12,000 in each of the twelve major systems of the body. We will explore this in more detail in our study of Revelation.

Reading 281-13 elaborates:

> With the arousing of this image, it rises along the Appian Way, or Pineal center, to the base of the brain... to those centers that give activity to the whole being... to the hidden eye... in the place just above the real face—bridge of the nose.

This "hidden eye" is the pituitary, also called the "third eye." *The Pineal's secretions—symbolically, the blood of the Lamb—purify the body.* The energies then move to the pituitary, from which healing prayers are sent as Cayce said, "on the wings of thought." These processes, described in Revelation, purify the body, balancing karmic distortions and replacing them with the pattern of the Christ. Thus, Babylon (the lower self) is replaced by the New Jerusalem (the higher self).

An old gospel chorus says, "There is power, power, wonder-working power in the blood of the Lamb." The Lord's Prayer contains symbolic references: "For thine is the kingdom" (thyroid), "the power" (Pineal), "and the glory" (pituitary). The rising energies flow through the centers, energized by the thyroid (Spirit center), and activate the Pineal—the seat of divine power.

Why, then, were bulls sacrificed in the OT? The bull, or calf, seen in Revelation, represents the first center—the reproductive glands. In Reading 294-140 we are told:

> The glands of reproduction... give up something that creation may be reached... The essence of Life itself is given in giving to another…

This is the meditator's sacrifice—channeling the reproductive energies upward in service of healing and transformation. Recall the story of the woman who touched Jesus' robe: "Jesus, immediately knowing in himself that virtue had gone out of him..." (Mark 5:30). Her faith allowed the release of His stored healing energy. The giving up or the release of that energy constituted a sacrifice.

In Voodoo and similar rites, animal blood sacrifice releases immense psychic energy. This may explain the primal attraction to bloodshed in ritual, hunting, or ancient arenas.

The energy released by OT sacrifices prepared the priest to enter holy spaces with elevated consciousness. The Bible requires the "first fruits"—the highest and best. In meditation, the "first fruits" are the reproductive energies, raised and redirected for sacred purposes.

Archetypal Mantras

The Lord's Prayer and the 23rd Psalm are archetypal mantras—templates for awakening the seven centers. The sequence of the 23rd Psalm mirrors that of the Lord's Prayer. When the Psalmist says, "Thou anointest my head with oil; my cup runneth over," this refers to the Pineal, the "golden bowl" of Eccles. 12:6. The Christ is the anointed one. The cup that runneth over is the activated Pineal.

The Readings say: "Keep the Pineal active and you will never grow old." It is a true fountain of youth. Recent studies, such as those cited by Steven Bock in *Stay Young the Melatonin Way*, suggest that melatonin—the Pineal's primary hormone—may help preserve genetic integrity by protecting telomeres.

The Lord's Prayer may be offered as outward petition or used as an inward mantra. In this mode, "Lead us not into temptation" becomes a call for the energies to rise inwardly, rather than flow outward into material distractions.

The tabernacle is thus revealed as an archetypal symbol of the Christ pattern—implanted within each of us, in bodies made in God's image. This inner pattern is one of perfect love. Just as we are born with the reflex to sneeze or cough, we are born with the divine blueprint to manifest perfect love. To become as Christ, as we were created to be.

The challenge before us is to choose this pattern as our ideal and to activate it through meditation and service. By doing so, we may truly become "gods, children of the Most High." (Psalm 82:6)

> Even the mystery which hath been hid from ages... which is Christ in you, the hope of glory. (Col. 1:26–27)

God's plan unfolds across time—through the OT tabernacle, the life of Jesus, and now through the temples of our own bodies. Each is a step in the return journey of the prodigal soul. Our bodies, designed to function in three dimensions, contain the circuitry needed to experience divine consciousness. This is our purpose.

The Bible is not just symbolic—it contains archetypes: universal patterns shared by all souls because we are created in God's image. These patterns often lie dormant. Like pregnancy, the capacity exists even if it is never expressed. The Christ archetype exists within every soul—but few ever activate it.

What is the practical value of these archetypes? Once activated, they unleash transformative energies. They can heal the seeker and empower that person to heal others. Charismatic leaders are not merely attractive—they are filled with the Spirit. Paul was transformed when the Christ archetype within him was awakened. His zeal activated the pattern that reshaped his soul and allowed him to understand the mystery: "Christ in you."

Morphic Resonance

How does the pattern of Jesus' life and sacrifice influence us as individuals? A deeper understanding of this indwelling pattern can be aided by Rupert Sheldrake's hypothesis of morphic resonance. Sheldrake presents research showing that if a group of rats is trained to solve a particular puzzle, then other rats—even in different parts of the world—can solve the same puzzle more quickly thereafter. He has demonstrated this astonishing phenomenon across various contexts. It is akin to striking a tuning fork at one frequency and causing other tuning forks of the same frequency to vibrate in resonance.

A well-known example of this is the breaking of the four-minute mile. Before 1953, it was widely believed to be physically impossible. When Roger Bannister broke that barrier, within the following year dozens of others did the same.

In this same way, the pattern of our god-beingness was implanted within us from the beginning, as we were made in God's image. Jesus lived this pattern out in fullness. Morphic resonance provides a framework for understanding how His example makes this divine pattern more accessible to all. As an archetypal symbol, this pattern can now be awakened in us when we hold an ideal of love and meditate on the truth of "Christ in you." This is how Jesus came "to save the world"—not through imitation, not through vicarious atonement, but by empowering us to become, through Him, the Christ beings we were created to be—children of the Most High, growing "unto a perfect man" (Eph. 4:13).

Sheldrake's work on morphic resonance also highlights the intuitive capacities of both animals and humans. In one compelling video, an African gray parrot engages in active telepathic conversation with its owner, offering a striking example of such inter-species resonance.

The Readings emphasize that meditation is vital. While we are incarnate in the earth—a three-dimensional realm—we possess a physical body, a mental body, and a spiritual body. For true soul development, these three must become attuned as One. The purpose of meditation is to bring the physical and mental bodies into harmony with their spiritual Source. This is accomplished through a threefold process: first, by establishing a spiritual ideal that reflects the soul's purpose; second, by dwelling upon that ideal in silence; and third, by applying the resulting attunement in service to those in need.

Attunement is related to vibration—a concept central to the Readings. Colors of the spectrum correspond to the seven spiritual centers. These are aided by musical notes, breathing techniques, chants, scents such as incense, and even specific stones or gems. These centers also correspond to the planets of our solar system and the dimensions associated with each. According to the Readings, between lifetimes on Earth we sojourn in the environs of these planets in consciousness. Many of our talents and predispositions are the result of such sojourns. A musician may have spent time in the sphere of Venus, a warrior in the energies of Mars.

Glands	Church	Lord's Prayer	Planets	Ancient Elements	Beasts	Opening Seals	Colors Music Numbers
Pituitary	Laodicea	Heaven / Glory	Jupiter	Love	Father	Silence	Violet (Golden)
Pineal	Philadelphia	Name / Power	Mercury	Light	Son	Upheavals (Earthquake)	Indigo (Purple)
Thyroid	Sardis	Will / Kingdom	Uranus	Life	Spirit	Souls Slain	Blue (Gray)
Thymus	Thyatira	Evil	Venus	Air	Eagle	Pale Horse	Green
Solar Plexus	Pergamos	Debts	Mars	Fire	Lion	Red Horse	Yellow
Lyden	Smyrna	Temptation	Neptune	Water	Man	Black Horse	Orange
Gonads	Ephesus	Bread	Saturn	Earth	Calf	White Horse	Red

Figure 13: A Rosetta Stone

Figure 13 is presented as a kind of Rosetta Stone for working with symbols, particularly in dreams. For instance, dreaming of water may suggest an association with the Lyden center and all its implications. The Reading 262-84 tells us, "The KEY should be making, compelling, inducing, having the Mind one with which is the ideal." In this way, the ideal is raised to activate the seven centers, awakening the pattern of the Christ within.

An interpretation of the Lord's Prayer was given specifically for this purpose. When asked whether the layout of the Lord's Prayer on their group's chart had any relationship to opening the centers, the response was:

> Here is indicated the manner in which it was given as to the purpose for which it was given; not as an only way but as a way that would answer for those that sought to be—as others—seekers for a way, an understanding, to the relationships to the Creative Forces. It bears in relationships to this, then, the proper place.

They then asked:

> How should the Lord's Prayer be used in this connection?

The answer:

> As in feeling, as it were, the flow of the meanings of each portion of same throughout the body—physical. For as there is the response to the mental representations of all of these in the mental body, it may build into the physical body in the manner as He, thy Lord, thy brother, so well expressed in, 'I have bread ye know not of.'

This explanation reveals how the Lord's Prayer can be used as a mantra. By addressing the Lord's Prayer and the 23rd Psalm parallels we can more easily see the archetypal aspects of these as mantras.

In the Lord's Prayer, the lower centers are addressed in this order: Gonads, Solar Plexus, Leyden (daily bread, forgive us our debts, lead us not into temptation). This order more accurately depicts the optimal sequence of activation. The 23rd Psalm follows the same archetypal pattern, yet it has one key difference. the lower centers are addressed: Gonads, Leyden, Solar Plexus.

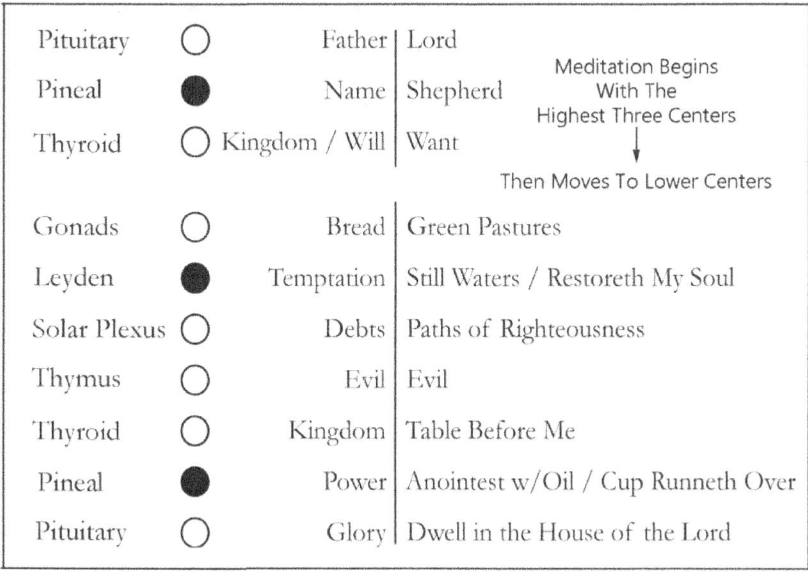

Figure 14: Archetypal Parallels of TLP and the 23rd Psalm

Jesus improved the sequence of the pattern in the 23rd Psalm when he gave the Lord's Prayer. Making the third center (Solar Plexus), come before the second center allows clearing the third center (lack of forgiveness) first. This way, the energy from the second center can rise on a purer path.

Even so, the overall process in both The Lord's Prayer and the 23rd Psalm is the same. The meditation process begins with the highest three centers, then moves to the lower four, and finally rises again through all seven. What's more, this same pattern is echoed in the classical mantra of Tibetan Buddhism: *Om Mani Padme Hum*. "Om" addresses the highest center, Oneness. "Mani" engages the mind. "Padma" refers to the lotuses, or centers. "Hum" raises the energy upward.

In the Revelation, the first church—Ephesus—represents the gonads. Its fault is that it "left its first love," referring to the Father, symbolized in the highest center. Thus, there is a natural affinity between the negative pole of the Lyden/gonads and the positive pole of the Pineal/pituitary. When the seventh center is awakened and the ideal is set in the Christ, the Pineal is activated, creating a natural draw that lifts energy from the first center upward.

Jesus said, "If I be lifted up like the brazen serpent in the wilderness, I will draw all men to me." (John 3:14). This is a reference to the raising of energy from the base of the spine—the kundalini or "serpent power"—which illuminates the seven centers when the ideal is set in Christ and meditated upon. This is the Way to Oneness. This is the path to developing spiritual gifts and psychic abilities. Though there are many gifts, there is but one Spirit—and only one Way to Universal Consciousness and union with God.

Clairvoyants like Theosophist C.W. Leadbeater have described the seven spiritual centers as vortexes of energy—wheels, or *chakras* in Eastern terminology. Anne Puryear began all her psychic work with an aura reading, which included examining the activity of each center. In her readings, blockages were often seen in the second, third, fourth, or fifth centers. The first and sixth centers were never blocked, though occasionally the seventh showed issues.

For example, a blockage in the third center—which relates to forgiveness in the Lord's Prayer—could prevent energy from rising further. If anger is retained, energy spills out in expression rather than rising upward. Similarly, the fourth center relates to self-gratification, the fifth to rebelliousness, and the second to sexual fixation. When these centers are blocked, energy cannot reach the pituitary to elevate consciousness or empower healing. Each line of the Lord's Prayer is directed at clearing a specific center, making way for healing energies to activate the transformative power of the pituitary—the center of the Father.

Because these centers vibrate, the Readings say music accompanies each opening—even if we do not hear it. The Readings also emphasize the near necessity of including music in our lives. We are encouraged to remain attuned to the music of nature and to make music ourselves—by singing, humming, or playing an instrument, even something as humble as a kazoo.

Shirley Winston's *Music Is the Bridge*, based on the Readings, is an invaluable resource. Anne Puryear was told psychically that birdsong in the morning is given to help awaken our spiritual centers and start the day in harmony.

CHAPTER 6
JESUS, THE WAY

FOR MANY GOOD reasons the man Jesus who became the Christ is truly the Way. Unfortunately, most of us associate Jesus with—and only with—Christianity. Out of respect for people of different religious traditions, and in an effort to be broad-minded, we sometimes group the leaders of the world's religions together, placing them on the same level. In truth, all of the great spiritual leaders belong to all of us. Jesus belongs to the world, not just to Christianity. In New Delhi, there is a great statue of Abraham Lincoln—he belongs to the world, not just to America. Gandhi belongs to the world, not just to India. All of the great leaders belong to all of humankind.

There are numerous belief systems. Is there an underlying truth? We should affirm—yes, there is.

Then the fundamental problem becomes clear: How may we know the truth? Any answer we offer may not satisfy the true believers of other traditions. A major part of the difficulty is that Christian theology itself is riddled with contradictions. We have addressed this at length. Let us begin, then, with our first premise: the Oneness of all Force. One reality, one Force, one

God, one truth. All of the eight billion or so souls incarnate on the Earth are brothers and sisters—divine beings—children of the Most High. As the Apostle tells us in Galatians 3:28, "There is neither Jew nor Greek, there is neither bond nor free, there is neither male nor female: for ye are all one in Christ Jesus." And as the old hymn rightly affirms, "In Christ there is no East or West."

We may not resolve the question of the centrality of the man Jesus who became the Christ in global religious discourse. However, our concern here is with the psychology of the soul. And in this realm, we have every reason to affirm that the archetypal pattern of the high self—the soul—is the same within each of us, as we are all made in the image of God. Its expressions may be shaped by culture, but the Readings declare that no soul has yet lived a life of selfless love in such fullness and perfection as Jesus. Through processes like morphic resonance, the divine pattern realized in Jesus' life is now available to each of us. It may awaken in anyone, though it may not always be described in Christian terms.

Our central premise is that the man Jesus fully embodied the divine pattern that is planted within us all. God is love, and we—God's children—are designed to become and to be beings of love. The Way, then, is the way of aspiration, attunement, and application.

In the teachings of Jesus, we learn that God is love, and the Way to Oneness with God is through love. We are called to love God, our neighbors, our fellow souls, ourselves—and even our enemies. On this last point, the Readings issue surprisingly strong warnings: unless we can perceive the love of God even in the vilest emotions, we have little grasp of what true love means.

The life of the Master was a life of pure, selfless love. We don't see that same level of selfless love manifested in the lives of other great teachers. Mohammed was a warrior. The Buddha was married with a child and left to pursue his spiritual path. We're not saying Christianity is superior to Islam, but we can say Jesus led a more perfectly loving life than Mohammed.The key insight here is that it is not dogma or religious belief that matters most. As the Bible reminds us, even the demons believe. What matters most is the spirit in which we live and express love in our relationships. A selfless Hindu mother nurturing her child may be more in tune with the Spirit than a self-absorbed "Christian" mother. We are all on the same ladder of growth—some higher, some lower. Thus, the Readings caution against criticizing anyone for where they are on that path.

Spiritual History

The Cayce Readings present a rich spiritual history of God, of His children, and of creation—insights found nowhere else. A brief summary of this account follows:

Out of a desire for companionship, God emanated souls from His own Being. These are His children. As in the parable of the Prodigal Son, we strayed by choice, even while still in celestial, spiritual form. To help us see the consequences of our self-centeredness, God manifested the material universe—emanating it from His own essence. Then He devised a path for us to become aware of our oneness with Him and the way of love.

There is soul entanglement throughout the universe. One group of souls—including us—entered the various planes of consciousness within this solar system. On Earth, our creations became more and more misaligned with God and love. As we projected ourselves into evolving life forms, some became increasingly distorted. The spiritual Forces then began to shape a vehicle that could survive on Earth—because that's where we had become trapped—and, at the same time, serve as a vessel in which the soul could remember its divine origin and experience reunion with the Father. Thus, God and His helpers developed homo sapiens.

The soul we now know as Jesus participated in this immense process, helping to create a suitable lifeform—homo sapiens—through which we could find our way back. This same soul was first known as Adam, the first soul to manifest in human form. The Bible refers to Adam as the "son of God" (Luke 3:38).

We know the story from there: Adam succumbed to temptation. But what we may not know—though it can be inferred from the Bible—is that this same soul, Adam, continued His mission through successive incarnations.

The Readings tell us that Adam had no birth, only a physical death. In Enoch—who "walked with God"—there was a physical birth but no death. In Melchizedek, there was neither a birth nor a death; he was "without beginning or end." At this stage, the soul realized that to be universally accepted, it would have to pass through the full range of soul experiences. Thus came Joseph, Joshua, Jeshua, and ultimately Jesus—with both a physical birth and death. The archetypal pattern was completed through His life, death, and resurrection—and is now fully available to every soul.

Through this perfect life of love, Jesus conquered death and revived His body in the resurrection. His resurrected body was a glorified one. According to the Readings, "glory" means the capacity to serve. The resurrection was not merely a fitting end to a sacred story—it was the beginning of a far greater work. As seen in His post-resurrection appearances—counseling the travelers to Emmaus, preparing breakfast for His friends on the shore—He continued to serve in His glorified form.

Christian theology speaks of our resurrection but rarely in terms of service. The Readings say that the pattern set by Jesus enables us also to develop glorified, resurrected bodies—for the higher purpose of loving service to others. These truths have profound implications for understanding the psychology of the soul and its journey toward Oneness.

The Psychology of Life

A seeker once asked the Cayce Source for a recommendation on the best book on psychology. The reply was: "The Gospel of John, which is the psychology of Life" (452-6). This gospel opens with the profound assertion: "In the beginning was the Word, and the Word was with God, and the Word was God… All things were made by Him… And the Word was made flesh and dwelt among us" (John 1:1, 14).

Let us affirm that God is not a moralist, as Christianity has often portrayed Him through its heavy emphasis on sin. Rather, God—as Jesus exemplified—is more of a psychologist. When the commandment says, "Thou shalt not covet," it is not because God is offended by the act of coveting. Instead, it is because a covetous spirit hinders one's happiness and spiritual attunement. It blocks the flow of love and stalls soul development. As 1 Corinthians 12:31 says, "…covet earnestly the best gifts…"—which means we are to long for divine love, not material possessions.

A psychological reading of the Bible yields far more applicable spiritual insights than a moralistic one. A miracle is a past event to be believed. An analogy, on the other hand, is a present truth to be applied.

The Gospel of John, as a psychology of life, is rich with truths and deserves careful study. There's no adequate way to summarize it fully, but for our purposes, we can highlight and comment on selected chapters and verses. The best approach is to read the entire gospel alongside the Bible, verse by verse, referring to the following insights as companion reflections.

John 1:29, 36 – John the Baptist calls Jesus "the Lamb of God." This becomes foundational for understanding the saving power of Christ's life and blood—the raising of Spirit to the Christ center within us, the Pineal.

Chapter 2 – Jesus turns water into wine at a wedding feast. Symbolically, this reflects the raising of spiritual energy from the second center (associated with water) to the sixth center, transforming into wine—His blood. The union of Lyden and Pineal forces is the symbolic inner wedding.

Chapter 3 – In His conversation with Nicodemus, Jesus says, "You must be born again." This clearly refers to reincarnation. A full case for this is made in *Why Jesus Taught Reincarnation.*

Chapter 4 – Speaking to the Samaritan woman at the well, Jesus invites her to partake of His "living water" and never thirst again. According to the Readings, this water is the energy raised from the Lyden (second) center. More broadly, the "water of life" also represents the manifestation of God as time, space, and patience—three dimensions of God's material expression. Jesus is this water of life.

Chapter 5 – Jesus calls God His Father, making Himself equal with God—an act for which He is later crucified. But He extends this same divine kinship to all of us, calling us children of God. He even says, "Is it not written in your law, I said, Ye are gods?" (John 10:34).

Chapter 6 – The multiplication of loaves and fishes demonstrates the creative power of the first and second centers. Jesus declares, "I am the living bread… Except ye eat the flesh of the Son of man and drink His blood, ye have no life in you." While this disturbed many, He clarified, "It is the spirit that quickeneth; the flesh profiteth nothing: the words I speak unto you, they are spirit, and they are life." We each must answer the question He then posed to the Twelve: "Will ye also go away?"—to which Peter replied, "Thou hast the words of eternal life."

Partaking of His flesh and blood is symbolic of activating the divine archetypal pattern within ourselves. As will be explored further, His flesh and blood represent the essential union of Lyden and Pineal energies. The statement "Except you eat… and drink…" is a call to inner transformation through attunement.

Chapter 7 – At a feast, Jesus says, "He that believeth on me… out of his belly shall flow rivers of living water." This again refers to spiritual energy rising from the Lyden to the Pineal center. The parenthetical note—"(But this spake He of the Spirit…)"—clarifies it's symbolic, not literal. Still, some denominations take this as evidence for literal transubstantiation. But Jesus always taught in parables. True transformation occurs within us when we receive the Eucharist in a spirit of love and surrender.

Chapter 8 – Jesus refuses to condemn a woman caught in adultery, urging us toward full forgiveness. One such woman was Mary Magdalene, sister of Martha and Lazarus. According to a Cayce life reading, she later became a resource for Jesus's followers. Though some claim Jesus married her, the Readings deny this, saying He would never have related to her in that way.

Later in the chapter, Jesus says, "Before Abraham was, I am." This links Him to Melchizedek, who served bread and wine to Abraham and received tithes from him (Gen. 14:18).

Chapter 10 – Jesus says, "I am the good shepherd... other sheep I have which are not of this fold... and they shall hear my voice." Like the shepherd who seeks the one lost sheep, He affirms His intention to bring all souls into Oneness, regardless of religious background. When He declares, "I and my Father are one," He is again charged with blasphemy. Yet, He reminds them, "Is it not written in your law, I said, Ye are gods?" (John 10:34, citing Psalm 82:6). This is the very truth for which He was crucified—and yet it is still denied by Christian theology today.

Chapter 11 – The story of Lazarus is confirmed in the Readings as a true resurrection. Lazarus, along with Mary, received their own Cayce Readings.

Chapter 13 – At the Last Supper, Jesus washes His disciples' feet and tells them, "Ye also ought to wash one another's feet." This humble act, when practiced, can be a deeply moving experience. The Readings pose a profound question: "Who was the greatest—He who made the worlds or He who washed His disciples' feet?" They remind us that, in the material world, only the little things matter.

Jesus then gives a "new" commandment: "That ye love one another." Loving others isn't new—but what is new is the phrase, "as I have loved you." This is said in a profound context: just before, Judas had betrayed Him; just after, Peter would deny Him. Thus, we are to love even those who fail or betray us. This command is repeated in John 15:12.

The 14th through 17th chapters of John are profoundly important. The Cayce Readings highly recommend that these be read as though the Master Himself is speaking directly to each of us. This is an invitation to hear with the ears of the soul.

John 14:2 – Jesus says, "In my Father's house are many mansions." This refers to many dimensions or states of consciousness. He continues, "I go to prepare a place for you"—not just in heaven, but across the many planes of our soul's journey. Just as He prepared the way in the three-dimensional Earth, He also prepared pathways in other dimensions of our solar system, shown symbolically below. Figure 15 shows types of consciousness during the planetary sojourns and in the interim between incarnations. Jesus manifested perfection in all of these sojourns.

Father	○	Jupiter	Universal Consciousness
Son	○	Mercury	Mind
Spirit	○	Uranus	Psychic
Air	○	Venus	Love
Fire	○	Mars	Wrath
Water	○	Neptune	Mystical
Earth	○	Saturn	Insufficient Matter

Figure 15: Types of Consciousness in the Planetary Sojourns

> **John 14:9–12** – To Philip, Jesus says, "He that hath seen me hath seen the Father." The Readings affirm that, in the Earth plane, the Father is represented by the physical whole. Jesus adds, "The Father that dwelleth in me, He doeth the works. He that believeth on me, the works that I do shall he do also; and greater works…"

This remarkable promise points to the potential within each of us. When the Father—the highest force, the Source—is fully activated within us through the union of Lyden and Pineal energies, we too may perform the "greater works." The Readings teach that the Father in each of us is symbolized by the Pituitary, the highest gland, awakened through spiritual alignment and love.

John 14:16–17 – Jesus promises to send the Comforter, the Holy Spirit, “to bring all things to your remembrance.” This is not about remembering facts, but soul memories—recollections from many lifetimes, dimensions, and experiences. As the soul comes into full attunement, past-life memories, dreams, spiritual gifts, and previously dormant talents begin to emerge. The Readings identify this Comforter as the Spirit of Christ.

It is important to note that while Christian theology presents the Trinity as “three persons,” the Readings reject this notion. God is not a person, though we may have a personal relationship with Him. Nor is the Holy Spirit a person. God is the One Force—singular, eternal, and unifying.

John 15:12 – Jesus reiterates: “This is my commandment, that ye love one another, as I have loved you.” Again, the emphasis is on **how** He loved us—not selectively, not conditionally, but inclusively, even when betrayed or denied. His love transcends judgment and reaches even the lowest soul.

John 16:13 – He tells the disciples that the Spirit of Truth will guide them into all truth, declaring “things to come.” This suggests the development of intuitive or prophetic awareness—the awakening of soul faculties. These gifts emerge naturally as we become attuned to the Spirit and commit ourselves to lives of love and service.

John 17:21 – In His final prayer, Jesus says, "That they all may be one; as thou, Father, art in me, and I in thee… that they also may be one in us." This verse may be the most important of all. It affirms the ultimate goal of spiritual life—not separation or salvation in the future, but union in the present. Oneness with God, Oneness with each other. The psychology of the soul is not about judgment or division—it is about union, remembrance, and transformation.

John 15: Jesus says, "I am the vine, ye are the branches." This metaphor affirms an ongoing, organic relationship: we are not separate creations, but emanations—extensions—of the Spirit of Christ. It supports the emanation theory, as opposed to the doctrine of creation ex nihilo, which is foundational to traditional Christian theology.

In this passage, Jesus also calls his disciples friends, not servants, reinforcing the truth that we are of the same essence as He is. We are not inferior beings; we are companions on the same spiritual path.

John 16: When Jesus says, "It is expedient for you that I go away: for if I go not away, the Comforter will not come unto you," He is pointing to an essential truth: as long as He remains physically incarnate, people will continue to look outside themselves for divine help. His continuing presence would prevent the necessary inward turn toward discovering the Spirit of Christ within. He even warns that some will say, "He is over here" or "He is there," and instructs us not to go out after such claims. His entire mission was to awaken in us the awareness of our own divinity—the Christ within.

John 17: Jesus declares His mission plainly: "That they all may be one; as thou, Father, art in me and I in thee, that they also may be one in us… that they may be one, even as we are one: I in them, and thou in me, that they may be made perfect in one." This is one of the most powerful affirmations of Oneness in all of scripture and perfectly aligns with our foundational premise: the Oneness of all Force.

John 18: During His hearing before Pilate, Jesus says He came into the world "to bear witness to the truth." Pilate famously responds, "What is truth?" The Readings note that, at this question, many in the spirit realms gathered around to hear Jesus' reply. It is unfortunate that Pilate did not wait for the answer. The Readings do provide one: Truth is that which awakens within us an awareness of our divine nature. Symbolically, Truth is associated with the second spiritual center, the Lyden.

John 19: When Pilate tells Jesus he has power over Him, Jesus replies, "Thou couldst have no power at all against me, except it were given thee from above." This principle—that all earthly power is granted from above—is echoed throughout scripture and in the Readings. We are advised to "Give God a chance." That is, allow the karmic forces at play—particularly in leadership and governance—to unfold in God's time, not ours. The Bible says, "These things must come, but woe to him by whom they come."

Karma teaches us that people will meet the consequences of their actions, but we are not to be the agents of their suffering. Those in power are a reflection of the collective karma and consciousness of the people they lead. We are meeting ourselves.

God is both Love and Law. The Law—karma—is a form of love designed to awaken and redirect us. If a leader is abusing power, this is not only that leader's karma but the karma of those who empowered him. When disasters strike and many suffer, some call it "the wrath of God." But God is not wrathful; God is love. Karma is not punishment. It is simply the lawful consequence of our choices.

If I build my house by a river, and the river floods, that is not punishment—it is natural law. Similarly, if I choose to incarnate on Earth, I must be prepared for impermanence and change. Harsh as it may seem, meeting the consequences of our choices is a gift from God, who desires that we turn from selfishness to the way of love. "Whom He loveth, He chasteneth." Heb (12:6)

Some ask: "Is it fair to suffer for a mistake I don't even remember making?" But our forgetfulness is of our own choosing. If someone commits a crime while intoxicated and does not remember it, are they blameless? No. Likewise, we have closed our eyes and ears to spiritual guidance. But when the Spirit comes, He will bring all things to our remembrance.

John 19:24 refers to the fulfillment of prophecy in the crucifixion of Jesus, especially as detailed in Psalm 22. His cry from the cross reflects an awareness that He was fulfilling His soul's purpose, as foreseen centuries earlier.

John 21: Jesus' post-resurrection appearance to the disciples at the Sea of Galilee must have been one of the most joyous celebrations in history. I call it "The High Five, Hang Ten Galilean Beach Party." In keeping with His nature, Jesus serves His friends—directing them to a miraculous catch of 153 fish and preparing a breakfast of fish and honey.

Fish, symbolizing water, point to the Lyden or water center; honey, symbolizing sweetness and Spirit, points to the Pineal, the Christ center. The Bible speaks of "honey from the rock." The Rock—always capitalized in the Old Testament—is a symbol for Christ, "the stone which the builders rejected." Why 153? The number 9 (1+5+3) symbolizes the completion of a mission. The resurrection of Jesus is among the greatest gifts humanity has received. And this breakfast of service and kindness affirms, as the Readings say, "in the material world, only the little things matter."

In this passage, Jesus also discusses the differing missions of Peter and John, as referenced in Revelation 10:9–11. Peter is to continue his work in the spirit realms, while John, through his advanced spiritual development, is to continue working on Earth through future incarnations: "Thou must prophesy again before many peoples, and nations, and tongues, and kings." This mission cannot be fulfilled in a single lifetime.

Finally, many today preach that simply confessing belief in Jesus as one's personal savior assures a place in heaven. But Jesus says otherwise in the Sermon on the Mount:

"Enter ye in at the strait gate: for wide is the gate, and broad is the way, that leadeth to destruction, and many there be which go in thereat. Because strait is the gate, and narrow is the way, which leadeth unto life, and few there be who find it." (Matthew 7:13–14)

Compare this to His parable of the sheep and the goats in Matthew 25:31–46. Not everyone who cries "Lord, Lord" will be heard. The Way is not about belief alone. It is about the life we live, the love we give, and the Spirit we embody.

CHAPTER 7
A Search for God

"Never doubt that a small group of thoughtful,
committed, citizens can change the world.
Indeed, it is the only thing that ever has."

~ Margaret Mead

The Cayce work was formally incorporated in 1931 as the Association for Research and Enlightenment. Soon after, members initiated a series of Readings for a group that came to be known as *A Search for God.* The first two Readings, given a week apart, responded to the group's request for a special message. They were told they were to present a light to a waiting world. The Reading emphasized practice over preaching. Then came this directive:

> "Be not unstable in things thou doest, for thou hast asked that thou be guided by that that may give a light to a dying world – not an individual, a world!" (262-2)

A dying world? What does this mean? In another series known as *The World Affairs Readings*, a critical turning point is identified at Versailles in 1922. Although many people opposed President Wilson, the Readings affirm that the Spirit of Christ sat with him at the negotiating table. This moment could have marked the end of all wars. Instead, the treaty was rejected due to "man's greed, man's fear," and, as the Reading laments, "soon there must be a reckoning. For again has the Prince of Peace been CRUCIFIED upon the ALTAR, the cross of greed!" (3976-16). This marked one of the early moments of the Apocalypse and is one reason why the group was called to present a light to a dying world.

What a profound challenge. In response, a series of 130 Readings—known as the *Study Group Readings*—was given. These Readings comprise one of the most important works to emerge from the Cayce material. The group was instructed to organize for the purpose of creating a program for soul development, designed specifically for spiritual seekers. A compiler later structured this material into a series of lessons—primarily twenty-four—which included the reported experiences of the group members themselves. The Source insisted that the members not only apply the lessons in their lives, but also share their personal experiences in the published materials. This experiential sharing, the Source said, would make the teachings more universally applicable. In this way, any study group could become genuinely effective.

This program became known as *A Search for God*, or ASFG. I like to refer to these ASFG lessons as *Learning How to Love.*

Each lesson offers a vital building block toward understanding and embodying love. For instance, Lesson One is *Cooperation*—a foundational quality of love. Jesus taught that love is the goal. I may not yet be able to fully love my neighbor, but I can become more cooperative. As I engage with the lessons—*Cooperation, Faith, Patience, Fellowship*—they unfold like petals on a flower, revealing the full blossom of love. This is the essence of soul growth.

The Source stated that few materials available to seekers are as valuable and helpful as these books—and that they will become textbooks for future generations.

Research has shown that small group work can have a more profound effect on personal growth than even individual psychotherapy. For such groups to be effective, they must share a common structure or content—such as the ASFG lessons—and encourage open sharing of personal experiences and insights.

The first section of the ASFG books presents a profound discussion on meditation. The affirmations provided with each lesson are intended to serve as focal points during meditation. Meditation is not optional in this work—it is essential. Some printings of the lessons oddly suggest that readers may skip the meditation section and proceed directly to the first lesson. This completely undermines the core purpose of the program. Meditation is central to the ASFG teachings.

The shared lessons provide structure, content, and continuity to group efforts, while the shared personal experiences fuel transformation more effectively than lectures or outside instruction. *A Search for God* combines these vital elements with a unique approach to meditation. Each lesson contains an affirmation expressing its central truth. When properly understood, these affirmations function as mantras.

Mantras

In his book *Foundations of Tibetan Mysticism*, Lama Govinda offers enlightening insights into the power of mantras. He writes:

> The power and the effect of a mantra depend on the spiritual attitude, the knowledge and the responsiveness of the individual. Mantras do not act on account of their own 'magic' nature, but only through the mind that experiences them. They do not possess any power of their own; they are only the means of concentrating already existing forces—just as a magnifying glass, though it does not contain any heat of its own, is able to concentrate the rays of the sun and to transform their mild warmth into incandescent heat. (p. 27–28)

Govinda's comment addresses the mistaken belief among some seekers that mantras possess intrinsic power. In reality, they focus and amplify the mind's intention. He further describes a specific type of extended mantra known as dharani:

> Dharanis are means for fixing the mind upon an idea, a vision or an experience gained in meditation. They may represent the quintessence of a teaching as well as the experience of a certain state of consciousness, which hereby can be recalled or recreated deliberately at any time. Therefore, they are also called supporters, receptacles or bearers of wisdom... Through deep absorption (samadhi) one gains a truth; through a dharana one fixes and retains it. (p. 31–32)

This is an ideal description of the purpose of the affirmations found in the ASFG lessons. The lessons themselves function as sacred texts; the affirmations distill their core wisdom. They are dharanis. For the ASFG lessons to fulfill their soul-growth potential, the use of these affirmations in meditation—as mantras—is essential.

We must remember: Cayce's Source stated that few resources available to seekers were as well-prepared or as significant as these ASFG materials. They are intended to become foundational textbooks for generations to come. Moreover, as Margaret Mead observed—and the Readings affirmed—a small group can indeed change the world. These ASFG groups were called to do just that.

CHAPTER 8
THE REVELATION

OUR UNDERSTANDING of the profound relationship between the soul and the physical body is significantly deepened through a series of Readings interpreting the Book of Revelation. In 1931, Edgar Cayce initiated a series of Readings for the ASFG (A Search for God) study group program. On the evening of the first Reading, Cayce had a dream in which he saw seven members of the group forming another study group, which would come to be known as the healing group. A subsequent Reading confirmed that the dream was indeed guidance, directing them to establish a new series of Readings. This group, calling themselves the Glad Helpers, became the focus of the 281 series.

The purpose of this group was to support and strengthen the broader ASFG movement. It proved to be a deeply significant and spiritually potent gathering. Several members were said to have lived during the time of the Master (Jesus): among them were Andrew the apostle, Mary and Martha (friends of Jesus), Lucius (bishop of Laodicea), the blind Bartimaeus (whom Jesus healed), one of the Holy Women, and a sister of the Samaritan woman at the well. Only one member had not lived during

Jesus' time but had known Him in a previous incarnation in Egypt.

This series of Readings addresses topics such as prayer, meditation, and the laws of spiritual healing. It includes eleven Readings interpreting the Book of Revelation and twelve focused on the function of the endocrine system. These two threads are profoundly interconnected, as many symbols in Revelation correspond to the functions of the endocrine glands. All of the Revelation Readings and the endocrine system Readings are available to seekers in John Van Auken's book, *Edgar Cayce on the Revelation.*

The Readings consistently emphasize the importance of self-study. One of the most effective ways to explore Revelation is to view each vision as symbolizing a structure or process within the human body as it seeks attunement with the Infinite. This attunement is not a one-time event but an ongoing spiritual journey. One seeker was advised: "…if you will read the Book of Revelation with the idea of the body as the interpretation, you will understand yourself and learn to really analyze, psychoanalyze, mentally analyze others. But you will have to learn to apply it in self first." (4083-1)

The Readings also recommend studying Revelation in parallel with *Gray's Anatomy.* A basic understanding of human anatomy and physiology is essential to grasp the rich symbolic meanings of the text. Ultimately, Revelation is meant to be experienced rather than merely understood intellectually. Here, we will highlight only a few of the most salient points.

We have already explored the archetypal nature of the Old Testament tabernacle's design and function. It consisted of three parts: the outer court, the holy place, and the holy of Holies. These areas correspond to the conscious mind, the subconscious, and the superconscious potential. A veil separated the holy place from the outer court, and another veil separated the holy of Holies from the holy place. Interestingly, the Kabbalistic Tree of Life also depicts two veils. The first corresponds to the Lyden (gonadal center) as an open or closed door; the second, the Pineal gland, is symbolized as an open door. This second veil is said to have been torn at the moment of Jesus' death, symbolizing that His completed mission granted us new access to the holy of Holies within ourselves.

Within the holy of Holies stood the Ark of the Covenant, which contained three sacred objects: the tablets of the law, Aaron's rod, and a pot of manna. The tablets represent the archetype of the Christ. Aaron's rod symbolizes the central pillar of the seven spiritual centers, and the golden pot of manna represents the energy of the Lyden or gonadal center. Through meditation, this energy may be elevated to the Pineal gland—the symbolic golden cup—referenced in Hebrews 9:4.

When Jesus said He had bread and meat "we know not of," He referred to the nourishment He received from these spiritual centers during meditation. According to the Readings, actual creation takes place during meditation. The immense power of the Ark mirrors the spiritual power that can be awakened within us when we activate the archetype of the Christ.

Another major object in the tabernacle was the menorah, located in the holy place. Standing five feet tall and made of solid gold, it held seven lamps and was designed with meticulous detail. One of the initial visions in Revelation presents a similar menorah, with seven lamps and a Christ figure walking among them. The Cayce Readings, along with other sources, interpret the seven lamps and seven churches as symbolic of the seven spiritual centers within the human body. These correspond to the seven endocrine glands, each linked to a specific plexus—such as the solar plexus with the adrenal glands. The menorah's purpose was to activate these centers in the priest as he approached the holy of Holies.

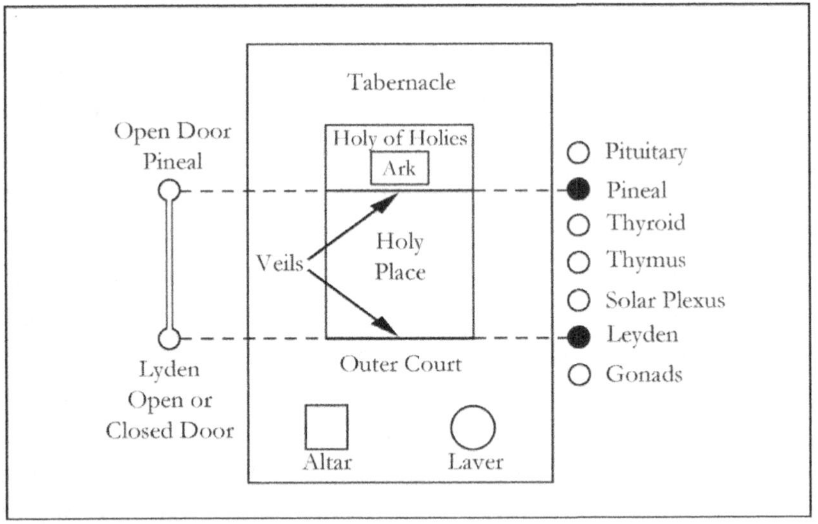

Figure 16: The Veils of the Tabernacle

In this detailed series of Cayce Readings, the connections between Revelation's symbolic visions and physiological counterparts in the human body are thoroughly explored. Both the symbols and the underlying processes—the anatomy and physiology—are archetypal in nature. Experiencing these symbols in sequence helps awaken and purify the spiritual centers, ultimately leading to expanded consciousness and a deeper capacity for service.

The theory behind activating these archetypes suggests that a profound spiritual awakening, like John's Revelation, may be accompanied by visions tailored to the seeker's state of attunement and inner realignment. Other seekers may also benefit by reading Revelation aloud—as encouraged by the New Revised Standard Version—and by visualizing the symbols. This practice can stimulate awakening, even without full intellectual comprehension. What is essential is the seeker's imaginative and emotional engagement with the symbols. This active response makes the process "mantric." Simply reading the text by rote or out of mere curiosity is unlikely to transform consciousness. The seeker must care deeply enough to internalize the symbols and activate the corresponding physiological centers within the body.

Archetypal symbols thus serve as a universal spiritual language, not requiring intellectual analysis but a responsive and seeking heart. As the saying goes, "a picture is worth a thousand words." By dwelling deeply on these symbolic images, we can unlock profound insights.

While intellectual understanding may help motivate a seeker, it cannot substitute for a dedicated imaginative engagement and a selfless spiritual intent. Only these qualities will energize the archetypal patterns. Simply "telling" your adrenal glands to activate will have no effect. Yet, entertaining thoughts of anger may quickly stimulate adrenal secretions. Similarly, dwelling on sexual fantasies activates the sexual glands. In the same way, meditating on the highest ideals—love and service—stimulates the pituitary, the highest endocrine center. With this foundational understanding, we can begin to explore the deeper meaning behind biblical symbolism. Immersing ourselves in the imagery and sequences of Revelation initiates profound attunement within the body.

The rituals of tabernacle worship were external enactments of internal spiritual processes that unfold within us during meditation. As with the Old Testament priests, these inner experiences can lead us to direct awareness of the indwelling Spirit of Christ. The tabernacle of the Old Testament and the New Testament's affirmation that "the body is the temple" reflect the unfolding evolution of humanity's understanding of God's purpose. Meditation is the key practice that allows us to align our physical and mental selves with our spiritual Source—our Father, God.

The Book of Revelation can be outlined as seven sequences of events experienced by John during his personal process of spiritual attunement. These same events and experiences are to be encountered by each individual during their own path toward awakening. The Cayce Reading offers *an* interpretation, not *the* interpretation.

The Revelation's purpose is foremost for the individual's personal transformation and application. That must come first. However, when individual experience is mirrored in the collective, we may also witness sweeping global upheavals—political, economic, and social. These events, symbolic of collective cleansing, mirror the inner purifications described in Revelation. Such challenges are unfolding even now. As Revelation describes the purification of the individual soul, we should expect parallel transformations on a global scale.

Ultimately, humanity must move beyond materialistic self-interest and theological dogma to a God-centered worldview grounded in the unity of all creation. Each person must grow from ego-centeredness to a realization of the spiritual kinship of all souls—children of the Most High.

Yet, this transformation will not be easy. The ego, both individually and collectively, resists surrender. What will it take for the wealthiest 1%—who control the majority of global resources—to become selfless benefactors of the poor? What will it take for rigid, exclusivist religious leaders to release their dogmas and embrace inclusive spiritual truth? What will it take for humanity to value cooperation over competition? What will it take for each of us to accept the truth that we are indeed "our brother's keeper"?

It may take a great and prolonged revolution—just as the Book of Revelation depicts. Both Jungian psychology and the Cayce World Affairs Readings warn that such changes may be imminent.

The Revelation outlines a path that leads us from limited human awareness to the realization of our full potential as spiritual beings—Christ-consciousness incarnate. Some believers expect to die, go to heaven, and be instantly transformed into perfect beings of love. But how can that be, if we resist love—especially love for our enemies—here and now? The Readings caution that "where the tree falls, there it will lie." We must not die angry. "That which we think continually we become…" and the soul feeds upon "that with which it will be possessed…" after passing. 3744-4. The Source reminds us: we don't go to heaven—we grow to heaven. Jesus said, "…strait is the gate and narrow is the way, which leadeth unto life, and few there be that find it." (Matthew 7:14)

The sequences of Revelation provide a spiritual roadmap for growth, attunement, and transformation. Along the way, we may encounter terrifying imagery. Yet even here, we are assured: "Fear none of those things which thou shalt suffer… be thou faithful unto death, and I will give thee a crown of life." (Revelation 2:10)

The seven sequences of the Revelation are processes that may be outlined as follows:

1. **Letters to the churches**: We are encouraged to examine our strengths and weaknesses in relation to the motivational functions of each of the seven endocrine glands. Each center is associated with a spiritual promise, granted when its limitations are overcome.

2. **The Lamb opens the seals**: The Christ within initiates the awakening of the centers, each accompanied by visionary experiences. The lower four centers are symbolized by the four horsemen.

3. **The sounding of the seven trumpets**: These herald the purification processes of the spiritual centers.

4. **Seven personages appear**: Beginning in Chapter 12, there is a shift in imagery. A woman in travail appears, and an encounter unfolds between Satan and the Archangel Michael. Michael protects the woman's child, symbolizing the birth of the Christ pattern within the seeker—a metaphor for a New Age or New Aeon.

5. **The seven vials and woes**: These represent the meeting and purification of karmic patterns and unresolved experiences from past lives and planetary sojourns.

6. **The destruction of Babylon**: This signals the dissolution of lower-self dominance and ego rulership.

7. **The establishment of the New Jerusalem**: This represents the emergence of the Higher Self—the divine promise of the soul's spiritual victory.

The fundamental commandments are to love God and to love our neighbor. These must be our foremost desire and guiding ideal. One way we manifest our love for others is by becoming instruments of healing for those in need. To serve more effectively as healing channels, we must understand the many factors addressed in this series of Readings given for the healing group.

The alignment and unification—attunement and at-onement—of our three bodies must be consciously sought if we are to become effective conduits for healing. Through meditation, we aim to harmonize the physical and mental bodies with the soul and with our divine Source. Healing can thus be defined in the same terms as meditation: it is the process of aligning the physical and mental with the Source. In order to do this effectively, we must understand the spiritual functions of our bodies, as revealed through this interpretation of the Revelation.

This framework provides us with insights into the extensive functioning of the endocrine system and how it is influenced by our desires, thoughts, and actions. These stages of attunement enable us to become powerful channels for healing—both of ourselves and of others. The following summary of the Revelation will become more meaningful if the reader refers to the corresponding verses in the King James Version of the Bible.

John tells us that he was "in the Spirit on the Lord's day." All the imagery that follows is thus a sequence of inner visions aligned with the meditative process of attunement in which he was engaged. These visions are intense and symbolic. From the beginning, we are assured: "Fear none of those things which thou shalt suffer." In this context, "suffer" may be understood as "experience." As we pursue our own inner revelation, we must not fear what we may encounter, however dramatic those experiences may be.

The opening vision is of the Christ figure walking among seven golden candlesticks. The lamps symbolize the seven spiritual centers within the body. The Readings stress that we are to view the endocrine functions as an interconnected system. The Spirit of Christ within us manifests at the center of these spiritual centers. This is analogous to the Old Testament depiction of God's presence among the cherubim on the Ark of the Covenant. It suggests an interactive and coordinated process among all the centers as a unified system.

Figure 17: John's Vision

The Christ figure holds seven stars—representing the seven spirits of God—in his right hand. He then places this hand upon John. This is a moment of deep significance. The angels of the churches symbolize the forces within the soul tied to its many potentials, shaped through experiences across multiple dimensions. When the Christ places his hand upon John's head, it signifies the soul's awakening by the Spirit to its journey through the dimensions of consciousness symbolized by seven of the planets of our solar system.

There are four beasts and twenty-four elders bowing before the throne. The beasts symbolize the four primary instinctual drives in the physical experience: sustenance (gonads), propagation (Lyden), self-preservation (solar plexus), and self-gratification (thymus). The elders represent the sensory system—the twelve bilateral cranial nerves, totaling twenty-four. In ordinary life, these drives and senses dominate and limit our awareness. But for true attunement, these lower forces must surrender their rule. They are excellent servants but poor masters in the operation of the higher three centers. Therefore, the four beasts and twenty-four elders must bow down, yielding their dominance in service to a higher spiritual ideal through the higher centers.

The Revelation then presents a sequence of seven stages. First, there are letters to each of the seven churches, identifying their virtues and shortcomings, along with promises for those who "overcome" at each level. Applied individually, this invites seekers to assess their own strengths and weaknesses relative to the desires and functions of these glands.

The first church, Ephesus, corresponds to the gonads—the source of the generative and reproductive life force. This center's energy remains vital throughout life. Its virtue is patience, which the Readings describe as an active spiritual force. Its fault is that it has "left its first love" (i.e., becoming one with the higher centers – with God). Ideally, the spiritual energy rises from this center to the seventh, the pituitary—the "Father" center. When that energy is depleted, such as through sexual excess, it cannot rise fully. The Father is love, and when our ideal is rooted in love, the energies of this center are drawn upward toward the seventh. Full transformation requires the energy from the gonads to ascend through each center until it reaches the highest.

The second center, the Lyden—represented by the church of Smyrna—is one pole of the Lyden-Pineal axis, which is considered the seat of the soul. Its message speaks of "poverty, but thou art rich," and promises "a crown of life" to those who overcome.

The third church, Pergamos, is the adrenal/solar plexus center, described as the place "where Satan's seat is." This refers to its association with anger and reactive power when misaligned.

The fourth church, Thyatira, corresponds to the heart center. It holds the virtue of love but is warned about the influences of Jezebel and fornication. To those who overcome, the "morning star" (Venus) is promised.

The fifth church, Sardis, linked to the thyroid and the Spirit aspect of the Trinity, is advised to "be watchful." According to the Readings, the thyroid is the most expectant and responsive of the seven.

The sixth church, Philadelphia, represents the Pineal gland—the Christ center. To the one who overcomes, it is promised, "I will make a pillar in the temple . . . and he shall go no more out." This center is associated with the Christ and the Lamb. It is notable that no fault is listed for this center, and it is called an "open door." Manly Palmer Hall interprets "go no more out" to mean an end to reincarnation.

The seventh church, Laodicea, symbolizes the pituitary gland. It is described as "lukewarm." While the pituitary has the capacity to direct the hormonal activity of all the other glands, when it lacks decisive engagement, more assertive centers like the solar plexus may dominate. The counsel is, "Buy of me gold!"—implying spiritual value. When the pituitary governs, the meditator experiences golden silence.

The next phase of awakening is the opening of the centers. John sees a sealed book that no one is worthy to open, until a Lamb with seven eyes appears. This Lamb, representing the Spirit of Christ, alone is worthy. The warning is clear: no one should seek to open these centers except through the Spirit of Christ—that is, with the highest spiritual intentions. Any attempt to force them open through artificial means, such as psychoactive drugs, is spiritually damaging. The seven eyes symbolize the seven centers, described in the Readings as psychic senses—hence, eyes upon the Lamb.

For example, a businessman might say he has a "gut feeling" about a decision. This could be a psychic perception originating in the solar plexus, tied to self-preservation. While it may be accurate, it may not serve the highest good for all.

The secretions of the endocrine system are extraordinarily powerful. When they are activated in disharmony—either with their function or with one another—they become destructive, leading to illness and behavioral imbalances. Hence, the caution.

As the four lower centers are opened, John sees four beasts: a calf, a man, a lion, and an eagle. The inclusion of a man is especially important, as will be explored further. These beasts symbolize the archetypal nature of the centers; the corresponding horsemen represent the active forces at work in them. The horse, symbolic of the messenger, conveys the hormones—each riding out to influence the entire body. Though these visions may seem violent, they represent the necessary purification of harmful patterns caused by previous misalignment. The horsemen thus signify a dynamic and necessary cleansing.

When the sixth center, the Pineal—the Christ center—is opened, there is an earthquake, representing the profound bodily changes initiated by Pineal activation. These powerful healing secretions are broadcast throughout the body, and they temporarily suppress the lower centers' reactive drives. Thus, four angels are said to hold back the winds—symbolizing the containment of lower impulses.

This period of inner quiet allows for the sealing of the 144,000 perfect cells in the body: 12,000 within each of the twelve major systems. These perfect cells, sometimes referred to as God's DNA, align with the archetypal blueprint for optimal functioning. Four of these systems are structural: bones, muscles, ligaments/tendons/joints, and skin. Four are vital for sustaining life: urogenital, digestive-eliminative, circulatory, and respiratory. Four are related to consciousness: lymphatic, nervous, sensory, and endocrine systems.

The body inherently knows how to heal. All any healing method can do is stimulate this natural intelligence. When the Pineal sends its attunement message, these 144,000 cells are activated, initiating deep healing. This process echoes the Biblical promise of the "power in the blood of the Lamb." John then sees a multitude dressed in white robes—those "who came out of great tribulation, and have washed their robes, and made them white in the blood of the Lamb."

It is important to stress: being "washed in the blood of the Lamb" is directly connected to the opening of the sixth center—the Pineal, the Christ center. Pineal secretions reach every cell in the body, activating their intrinsic pattern of perfect function.

The "blood of the Lamb," which brings salvation, is this rising life force from the Lyden to the Pineal—the seat of the indwelling Christ. When this energy activates the Pineal, its hormones circulate throughout the body, bringing healing, purification, regeneration, and transformation. We are thus quite literally saved by being "washed in the blood of the

Lamb." And so, the old hymn rings true: "There is power, power, wonder-working power in the precious blood of the Lamb."

Remember that in the Lord's Prayer, which addresses the three higher spiritual centers, we affirm: "For Thine is the kingdom"—corresponding to the thyroid; "the power"—the Pineal; and "the glory"—the pituitary, forever. Similarly, in the 23rd Psalm, the closing verses speak to these higher centers: "Thou preparest a table before me. I shall not want" relates to the thyroid; "Thou anointest my head with oil"—the word "Christ" meaning "the anointed one"; and "My cup runneth over"—a reference to the Pineal. The "cup" here aligns with the "bowl" of Ecclesiastes 12:6: "Or ever the silver cord be loosed, or the golden bowl be broken." The silver cord is the subtle thread connecting the Lyden to the Pineal. This connection is a vital key to understanding the power inherent in the "blood of the Lamb."

Cayce Reading 281-13 elaborates:

> The spirit and the soul is within its encasement, or its temple within the body of the individual—see? With the arousing then of this image, the ideal [which is the archetypal pattern of the Christ within] it rises along that which is known as the Appian Way, or the Pineal center, to the base of the brain, that it may be disseminated to those centers that give activity to the whole of the mental and physical being. It rises then to the hidden eye in the center of the brain (pituitary) system,

> or is felt in the forefront of the head, or the place just above the real face—or bridge of the nose, see? —281-13

The Readings use the word "disseminated" in two important ways. First, when "my cup runneth over," it signifies that the Pineal secretions are released and spread to every cell in the body, bringing healing, empowerment, and purification. This event, symbolized by an earthquake in the Revelation, marks a transformative moment. Second, once empowered, the energy rises to the "hidden eye"—the pituitary—enabling healing to be sent outward on the wings of thought to those we pray for. The Lord's Prayer concludes with the phrase "For Thine is the glory…" In the *Search for God* material (p. 215), glory is defined as "**the ability to serve**." Thus, our prayers, when offered in attunement, become powerful instruments of service.

When the life force rises and activates the Pineal, and the body is fully attuned, the pituitary becomes the agent through which healing is disseminated. To be "saved by believing on His Name" means raising the spiritual energies to the Pineal—the center we invoke in the Lord's Prayer as the sixth center.

Upon the opening of the seventh center, there is "silence in heaven for about the space of half an hour." This corresponds to the silence often experienced in deep meditation.

Several significant visionary experiences follow, which warrant commentary:

In relation to the opening of the fifth center—the thyroid, or Spirit center—the name Abaddon (or Apollyon) is given. Both names mean "the Destroyer." The deeper significance of this title will be explored later in connection with the Hindu deity Shiva. The thyroid governs metabolism, which includes both anabolic (building up) and catabolic (breaking down) functions.

In Chapter 11, John is instructed to "measure the temple." This command addresses the extent to which John's newly awakened consciousness encompasses compassion and acceptance of others. Will he serve all, or only a select group—perhaps only his own Jewish community? As we advance in consciousness, we too must ask: How inclusive is our service? The Readings lament that many denominations and creeds remain narrow and exclusive, resisting broader fellowship. We are reminded: "With what measure ye mete, it shall be measured to you."

In Chapter 13, a false prophet is introduced—one capable of performing miracles. This symbolizes a stage in personal development where psychic gifts are emerging, but the channel is not yet fully matured. Such information may be inconsistent or unreliable. In group study settings, individuals may begin to show psychic tendencies, and others may prematurely encourage them to give readings. This can delay or derail their deeper development. The false prophet represents a condition where the Lyden is active enough to access psychic impressions, but the overall system is not yet stable or fully attuned.

Much is made by doomsday prophets of the battle of Armageddon. More fruitfully, this battle can be understood as an internal conflict—the soul's struggle with its own rebellious nature. When this inner battle becomes widespread across humanity, we face large-scale apocalyptic challenges. Evidence of this can be seen in our world today. Jungian analyst Edward Edinger, in his important book *Archetype of the Apocalypse*, writes that this archetype is now "constellating," and that the world is entering a time of profound transformation. His book is essential reading for serious students.

Chapter 17 describes a beast that "was, and is not, and yet is." The symbolic meaning of this phrase can be illustrated through the archetypes presented in *The Wizard of Oz*, which will be explored in detail later.

In Chapter 20:10, the devil, the beast, and the false prophet are cast into a lake of fire to be tormented forever. Fire here symbolizes the adrenal/solar plexus center. When a seeker reaches a high level of attunement and integration, the solar plexus becomes so sensitized that it intercepts and neutralizes any disruptive impulses from the other centers before they are acted upon. For instance, if one is about to make an unwise choice, the thyroid's hormonal activity might be restrained by the solar plexus center.

Chapters 9 and 17 describe a bottomless pit. The path of love is direct and stable, but diverging from it leads to endless and unpredictable consequences—thus, a symbolic bottomlessness filled with unending and undesirable experiences.

Chapter 20 speaks of a 1,000-year period during which Satan is bound. This passage pertains to global rather than individual transformation. During this millennium of peace, only souls committed to doing no harm will be permitted to incarnate. The purpose of this era is to establish enlightened institutions—churches, schools, communities—that can support the spiritual development of those still evolving. When the thousand years conclude, Satan is "loosed"—meaning that previously unredeemed souls may again enter incarnation, this time within a more supportive and spiritually advanced society.

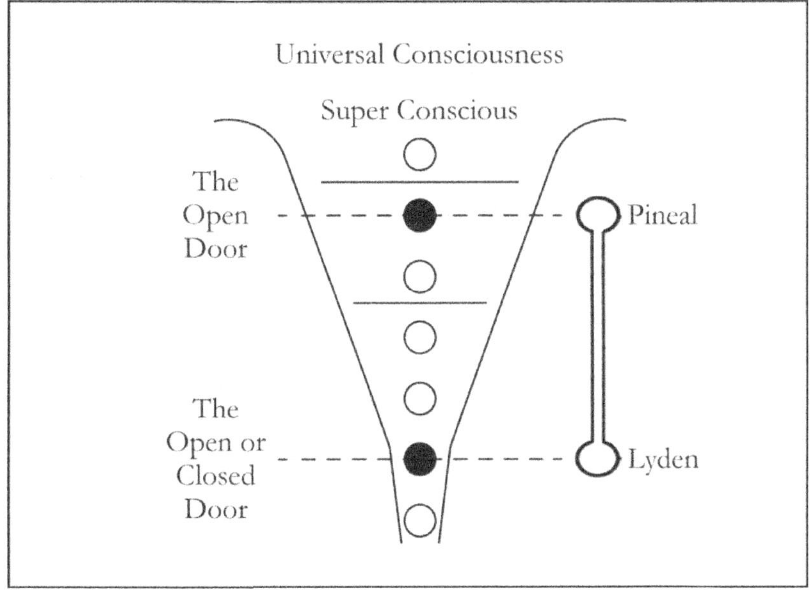

Figure 18: Path of the Rising Kundalini

When the kundalini energies are raised from the Lyden to the Pineal, they overflow to the body. The energy then rises to the

Pituitary/Father. This opens access to the Universal Consciousness.

At the opening of the seventh center, Revelation 8:1 declares, "there was silence in heaven about the space of half an hour." This reinforces the interpretation that the Revelation describes a deeply personal, meditative experience.

After this period of silence, John sees seven angels with seven trumpets. The visions that follow represent stages in the purification of the seven centers.

The Readings emphasize the importance of vibration. The human body is considered a microcosm of the universe—each element of the cosmos is mirrored within. Accordingly, the activity of the centers corresponds to musical notes, colors of the spectrum, and planetary influences on consciousness. Like Jewish mysticism, the Readings affirm the significance of numerology and the vibrational power of letters and numbers. The number of the beast is 666.

1	**2**	**3**	**4**	**5**	**6**	**7**	**8**	**9**
A	B	C	D	E	**F**	G	H	I
J	K	L	M	N	**O**	P	Q	R
S	T	U	V	W	**X**	Y	Z	

Here is an illustration relevant to current times: Notice that the letters F, O, and X, FOX, are 666, the Revelation's number for the number of the Beast. The numerological total is a 9 which signals an ending.

The mark of the Beast is revealed when a person prioritizes loyalty to societal norms and human expectations over fidelity to the Spirit. For example, a father may choose to keep his tee time with golfing friends instead of attending to his child's needs. A mother may neglect her responsibilities to her child in order to complete a bridge game. Politicians may cast votes that support their party rather than serving the greater good of the state or nation.

Numerical symbolism also plays a central role in the opening visions of John's Revelation and in the deeper, archetypal meaning embedded in the Lord's Prayer.

According to the Cayce Readings, each key phrase in the Lord's Prayer corresponds directly to one of the seven spiritual centers. This relationship is designed to activate the system during meditation. As the Readings describe it, one should feel "the flow of the meanings of each portion of same throughout the body physical." In this way, the Lord's Prayer becomes a mantric formula, revealing an archetypal pattern for deep meditative practice. Given our discussion of the Bible's archetypal structure, we can now look for parallels between the Lord's Prayer and other scriptural passages.

The beloved Twenty-Third Psalm, rich in poetic depth, is also archetypal in nature. Its language, sequence, and structure mirror that of the Lord's Prayer. Both texts address the higher three centers, then the lower four, and then return to the higher three.

The connection between the seven spiritual centers and the planets reflects the soul's sojourns through various dimensions of consciousness. The soul's journey does not unfold solely on Earth; it includes interim experiences in the consciousness realms represented by each of the planets in the solar system.

There is a profound and dynamic interplay between the soul and the physical body. Central to this process is the energetic flow between the second and sixth centers—the Lyden and the Pineal. The second center is referred to as the Leidig, named for its discoverer. Cayce called it the *Lyden*, meaning an "open" or "closed" door. The sixth center is the Pineal, which Cayce described as an "open door." The Pineal plays a critical role in awakening the system.

The pineal gland has a long and often misunderstood history. The Roman physician Galen (130–210 CE) called it the "first instrument of the soul." René Descartes (circa 1640) declared the Pineal to be the "seat of the soul." However, these insights were widely mocked by the scientific community. Because the concept lacked what was considered "scientific respectability," many researchers avoided studying the Pineal altogether to protect their reputations. Yet, the Cayce Readings offer rich and compelling information about the gland's relationship to soul activity. It seems Descartes and others intuited a profound connection between the soul and the Pineal. Their critics, failing to understand the metaphysical implications, dismissed these insights as superstition.

As shown in the Figure 12 under “Beasts”, two of the seven centers—the second and the sixth—bear the name of a man. Similarly, of the four beasts described in Revelation, three are animals and one is a man. The sixth center, symbolized by the man, is the center of the Son or the Christ.

The Silver Cord

The connection between the Lyden and the Pineal is especially intriguing. At the moment of conception, when the sperm and ovum become one cell, this single cell divides and extends, forming a long thread of nerve tissue from the lower body to the center of the brain—resembling the yin-yang dynamic of Taoism. Other cells then develop around this central thread. The Cayce Readings refer to this connection as the “silver cord” described in Ecclesiastes 12:6: “Or ever the silver cord be loosed, or the golden bowl be broken.”

The two poles of this original cell—and the cord connecting them—are described as the seat of the soul (Reading 294-142). It is through these centers that the soul, and the mind as an expression of the soul, manifest within the body. If the cord is severed, soul contact is lost and the body dies. If there is improper pressure on the cord, pathological or even hallucinatory experiences may occur.

In one Reading, the Lyden and Pineal are referred to jointly as one entity: the Pineal. At birth, the *function*—though not the structure—of these two poles is separated. As a result, the conscious mind loses direct access to the soul's ancient memory. The Genesis story of the fall explains this through the symbolism of a "flaming sword" placed in Eden to block the way to the Tree of Life. This corresponds to the veils in the Jewish tabernacle—symbolic of the separation between spiritual knowledge and waking consciousness.

Only through the *reunion* of these poles—most commonly during deep meditation—can the seeker regain full spiritual awareness and access to the latent gifts of the soul. Tibetan Buddhism refers to this as the Great Straight Upward Path, or the Great Perpendicular Path. In Hindu practice, the sushumna nadi represents this vertical channel, flanked by ida and pingala. In the Kabbalistic Tree of Life, the central pillar also symbolizes this path. The Readings call it the Appian Way or the silver cord.

While incarnate on the Earth plane, the soul slumbers and dreams, according to the Readings. Yet even in that sleep, we remain accountable for the choices we make. We live in a state of submerged memory, often puzzled by the consequences of our own past creations. Both our undesirable karmic patterns and our earned gifts and talents are buried in the subconscious—the mind of the soul. When the energies of the Lyden rise, powered by the first center (the gonads), and reach the Pineal, the soul awakens to its full potential: Universal Consciousness—the state Cayce accessed in giving the Readings. As promised in Scripture, when the Spirit comes, all things are brought to our remembrance.

The Marriage in Heaven

In Revelation, four beasts are described. The second center is symbolized by a man, indicating its unique role relative to the other three. The sixth center represents the Son, the Christ. Symbolically, these two centers reflect the polarities of energy: positive and negative, masculine and feminine. Their union in meditation signifies the spiritual marriage depicted in Revelation—the joining of the *church as bride* and *Christ as groom*. The Song of Solomon expresses this same theme poetically: the intimate beauty of archetypal spiritual union.

These archetypal dynamics appear throughout world literature, folklore, and religion. In the fairy tale Snow White, the Seven Dwarves represent the seven centers. Snow White symbolizes one pole of the soul. Like Eve, she consumes forbidden fruit and falls into a deep sleep. Only the kiss of the Prince—symbolizing the Christ or higher soul pole—can awaken her into full consciousness. We say:

Our Father (pituitary), which art in heaven Hallowed be Thy NAME … (pineal).

Thus, when we pray "in His Name," it is not merely a verbal formula—it is a spiritual alignment. For there to be power, the spiritual energies must rise to the Pineal.

CHAPTER 9
ONTOGENY AND THE ORIGIN OF EVIL

AS WE EMPHASIZE the Oneness of all Force, we encounter a profound enigma: How are we to reconcile the origin of evil with the inherent goodness of God? We know that God is love, and yet much of our human experience reveals the opposite. The Cayce Readings address this paradox: "yet the other side or the reverse of love is suffering, hate, malice, injustice. It is the reverse. Why?" (EC 281-51)

The Readings offer a profound and unexpected insight. But they also caution us that this truth will be difficult to grasp. We are warned that it will demand deep study and reflection:

> ...let that which is given here and now NOT become confusing. For, it will require deep meditation upon such, that you may get the correct insight; which you will not be able to put into words at first, and will KNOW when you know, but [only] by the experience of coordinating physical, mental and spiritual attributes into one.

The Readings add a further caution:

> ...much study, much meditation is needed here. Much has been given. As it is better understood, papers may be prepared on same which would prove not only interesting but most beneficial.

What is this new insight? Let's explore more deeply.

There is a well-known phrase in biology and anthropology: "Ontogeny recapitulates phylogeny." This theory suggests that the development of the individual mirrors the evolutionary development of the species. A similar pattern appears in the macrocosmic development of God and the microcosmic development of individual souls. According to the Readings, God created souls—His children—out of Himself, driven by a desire for companionship. This longing, however, required *a consciousness of separation.*

Therefore, souls made in His image carry within them both a consciousness of separation and a desire for companionship beyond themselves. What occurred at the cosmic level with God continues at the individual level each time a soul prepares for physical embodiment. A longing for self-expression outside of oneness appears both in God's initial act of creation and in the soul's own emergence into the world. In both Creator and creature, we witness the tension between unity and separation.

At the microcosmic level, while still in spirit, this desire for self-expression led to attempts to create and express outside the bounds of God's law of love. In its most extreme form, this constituted a spirit of rebellion—a fall in heaven, so to speak. Isaiah 14:12–16 depicts this problem: Lucifer, referred to as a man (a son, not an angel), declares, "I will be like the most High." The Readings suggest that some souls have, since the beginning, intended to do evil. "He was a murderer from the beginning …" (John 8:44) It seems as though some souls, at the very second that they realized that they had free will, chose to do other than what they knew to be God's will. Just as God created us out of His desire for companionship, so apparently some wanted to be gods apart from God.

Scripture also refers to Belial: "And what concord hath Christ with Belial? Or what part hath he that believeth with an infidel?" (II Cor. 6:15). There are at least twenty Old Testament references to the sons and daughters of Belial, indicating that this strain of souls—intent on evil—has existed for millennia, perhaps even millions of years. The Readings mention individuals who, in past lives (such as during Atlantis), were associated with this group. Though these souls may cause chaos, they are not eternally condemned.

It is essential to grasp the profound parallel between God's creation of souls and a parent's conception of a child. Just as God creates souls from Himself, parents generate a new being from their own substance. This act provides an opportunity for a soul to enter for self-expression.

This division—these opposing desires within the soul—manifests on a microcosmic level at the moment of conception, when the fertilized egg divides into two centers: The Lyden and the Pineal. This cell division marks the seat of the soul in its new incarnation. The Lyden and Pineal maintain a shared oneness in structure but remain distinct in function and desire. The Readings refer to this ongoing dynamic between the Lyden and Pineal as the "long thread activity."

From its initial entrance into the physical realm, the unenlightened soul possesses only a sense of SELF. This SELF-awareness constitutes the root of sin. The soul perceives the world through the Lyden, but it does not attain full Christ-consciousness until the energies of the Lyden rise into harmony with the Pineal. The lower self, marked by separation and egotism, may persist across many incarnations. Only when the soul, like the Prodigal Son, recognizes its estrangement and seeks reunion with the Divine can transformation begin: "I will arise and return to my Father's house."

God is love, and the soul's return to unity with the Father requires embracing the fundamental law of love. We must love God with all our heart, mind, and soul. Until this union is achieved—both consciously and unconsciously—every incarnation will reenact this division at the moment of physical formation. True reunification with God must involve conscious effort, deepened by profound meditation. This requires a reunified oness of the Lyden/Pineal relationship. Remember: the seat of the soul is in this relationship.

Reading 281-51 presents these complex concepts, beginning with a question that introduces a remarkable revelation:

Is the First Cause, then, that the separation of God in the desire for companionship with Himself, that as created or brought into a material manifestation the reverse of love, of hope, of patience, of all the attributes that are the spirit of activity, the moving influence or force? This we see in a physical body through the glandular system—as the activity of conception, the dividing of the activity of the gland itself, that brings conception.

Thus, this is the first of the centers from which arises all that is movement, to bring into being both the face and the preface—or the back, or the reverse—in the experience. It carries with it, what? That MIND! For, remember, ever, the pattern is ever the same—Mind the builder!

Conceived, then the first movement is along that center or gland (Lyden) which either fades or becomes a channel along which there may move the power and might to find expression through the very activities of the organs of the body itself.

Then the next is the Pineal, through which the brain forces make manifest . . . that held by the INDIVIDUAL separation and COMBINATION of the activity of the glands in that period of conception. Hence there arises . . . the figure of that beheld by that choice in its activity as it has separated itself from the first cause, or first premise; by the very will of the Father-God in the beginning.

This reading refers to "the face and the preface—or the back, or the reverse." A biblical echo of this idea is found in Exodus 33:23, where Moses pleads to see God's face. The Lord replies that no man may see His face and live. Yet, God places Moses on a rock, covers him with His hand, and as He passes, says, "I will take away my hand, and thou shalt see my back parts: but my face shall not be seen." Similarly, we today may not see God's face, but we may glimpse His "back parts"—the preface or reverse side. This image may help conceptualize the surprising revelation in the Readings.

At the moment of conception, the cell begins to become polarized, developing the Lyden and Pineal as one cell connecting the two poles by the Silver Cord, the "threadlike" connection of the two.

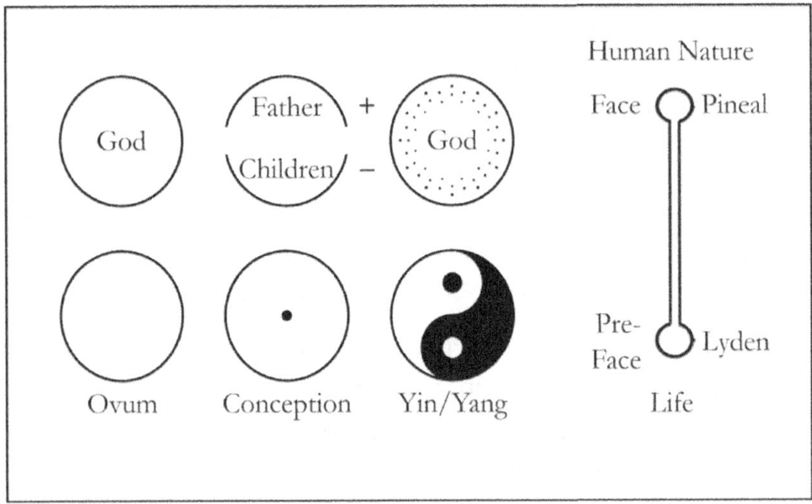

Figure 19: The Moment of Conception

These challenging lessons continue as the Readings discuss the fall on Earth, following the fall in heaven:

> WILL—with the environmental forces and the spiritual negative in the serpent—acceded to desire, to become and to experience IN that kingdom of influence. This brought acceptance, by man's own will. (281-54)

An interpretation of this might read as follows: After the spiritual fall, God created the material world to provide fallen souls a space to experience the consequences of their imbalances. This world was not created for our permanent residence, but for our learning. The spirit realm rejoiced when Earth became habitable, for it offered a school for the soul.

The soul who became Adam had earlier experiences on Earth, though not yet in physical incarnation. God created Homo sapiens by modifying patterns from existing life forms—resulting in a new, perfected body suitable for Adam. This body contained all that was needed.

In Eden, the serpent is called the "spiritual negative." This force originated from the same separation in God's creation of souls. We see a similar impulse in Adam's desire for Eve, who—as the story of the rib suggests—was in fact a part of himself.

Thus, the Readings draw a direct parallel between God's longing for companionship through soul creation and a parent's desire for companionship through childbearing. At the moment of conception, a polarity is established. This separation—within God and within each soul—is best understood in terms of vibration and polarity rather than in purely moral terms. The Reading cautions: we may gain "the correct insight, only by the experience of coordination of the physical, mental, and spiritual attributes into one." Therefore, we must consider the physical process of conception, especially the Lyden/Pineal polarity it sets into motion.

The discarnate soul—out of harmony—enters a polarized channel that reflects and reinforces its internal division. As earlier noted, the root problem is SELF. From the first division of embryonic cells, consciousness is rooted in the self-oriented or negative pole (Lyden) rather than the positive pole (Pineal), which holds the potential for Christ-consciousness. After the fall in heaven, this polarity was embedded in the soul, expressing both the desire for self-will and for alignment with God's will. The Lyden holds the lower self; the Pineal holds the potential higher self, activated through high ideals and deep meditation.

Let's now return to the ontogeny/phylogeny relationship. God, desiring companionship, emanated souls from Himself. This is mirrored in parents who, through conception, bring a child into being. God's act required a consciousness of separation. Similarly, earthly parents, in their longing for companionship, enact the same pattern. The soul that enters the body carries its own desire for expression, distinct from the consciousness of the parents.

Only through deep meditation can we raise the soul's energies and achieve the highest desire: unity within ourselves and with

God. The condition of separation—manifested even in the embryo—finds a close parallel in spiritual teachings such as those found in *The Secret of the Golden Flower*.

CHAPTER 10
THE SECRET OF THE GOLDEN FLOWER

THE SECRET OF *The Golden Flower* is an ancient Daoist text rooted in over a thousand years of Chinese mysticism. Carl Jung held both the book and its translator, Richard Wilhelm, in high regard, describing them as among the most profound influences in his life. Throughout this chapter, we will abbreviate *The Secret of the Golden Flower* as SGF.

The Cayce Readings emphasize that we grow in understanding through comparison. I once mentioned the SGF during a meditation workshop, only to have a woman later confess, "When you brought that up, I stopped listening. I don't want to hear about anything but the Readings." Yet this attitude runs counter to what the Readings encourage. Consider the following guidance given to a forty-nine-year-old woman:

(Q) What should I do to advance my spiritual growth?

(A) As just indicated, an analysis and a correlating of similarities—not differences—in the teaching of the many that are called sects, sets, or teachings of the varied portions of the UNIVERSE today. For practical application. WHY the Laplander or the Icelander or the people of Greenland or the Eskimos hold to certain legends, and as to WHY these find some parallel and comparison to those legends held by those in New Zealand, and off the coast of the South Seas

WHY the teachings of a portion of the peoples in the Persian land, the first of those great teachers historically recorded, compare or parallel with the Indians in the southwest portion of America.

Or WHY the teachings of Confucius or his axioms and lessons, and those of Jesus, are parallel.

Not their differences, but their overlapping. And what these teach in the many varied sects, the many varied cisms — not their differences but their unity. These will not only enable the entity to give to others but in the giving, in the seeking, in the understanding, broaden — yea, magnify — the vision and the ability in spiritual things. (473-1, p. 61)

As the Readings urge us to consider *why* these similarities exist, we may begin to understand: they are the result of universal archetypal patterns within human consciousness. These patterns manifest in the diverse ways humanity seeks meaning and understanding.

Let's now explore some of the parallels between the Readings and the SGF concerning the soul's separated condition.

I have often found that if one does not first understand the question, one may not recognize the answer. The Readings raise profound questions about the soul's origins. The SGF offers enlightening insights that parallel and illuminate those questions.

As noted earlier, Carl Jung—perhaps the most influential psychologist of his era—was deeply moved by Wilhelm's translation of the SGF. In his commentary, Jung presents a significant challenge:

> In the Pauline Christ symbol the deepest experiences of the West and the East confront each other. Christ the sorrow-laden hero, and the Golden Flower that blooms in the purple hall of the city of jade—what a contrast, what an infinity of difference, what an abyss of history! A problem fit for the crowning work of a future psychologist! (p. 133)

In this chapter, we attempt a beginning response to Jung's challenge. His concern appears rooted in the cultural divide between East and West, particularly between Daoist mysticism and Christian theology. Yet, a careful reading reveals that the Pauline Christ symbol and the imagery of the SGF are not incompatible. In fact, it may be through the insights of the Readings that this perceived chasm can be bridged. The bridge lies not in theology but in the Readings and in scripture.

The parallels between the SGF and the Readings are rich and illuminating. Each deepens our understanding of the other. Both sources resonate with the archetypal language of the collective unconscious, the very realm in which Jung specialized. It is curious that Jung never fully explored the archetypal connections between the Christ figure—what he called the archetype of the Self—and the archetype of the Golden Flower. Perhaps Western theological limitations prevented him from doing so. From my perspective, however, the parallels are striking—perhaps even identical.

Both the SGF and the Readings begin with the Oneness of all Force. Both affirm that the human body is a microcosm of the universal macrocosm. Both insist on the vital necessity of meditation for spiritual evolution. And both stress the importance of self-understanding. Significantly, each identifies the same bodily systems and centers involved in meditation.

Just as Christ is described as the Light of the World, so too is the Golden Flower identified as the Light. In the Readings, the upper three spiritual centers are emphasized. In the SGF, the "heavenly heart"—corresponding to the pituitary gland—is a central symbol. The SGF states:

> In the square inch field of the square foot house, life can be regulated. The square foot house is the face. The square inch field of the face: what could that be other than the heavenly heart? . . . The heavenly heart is like the dwelling place—the light is the master... Therefore, when the light circulates, the energies of the whole body appear before its throne, as when

> a holy king has established the capital and has laid down the fundamental rules of order, all the states approach with tribute... Therefore, you only have to make the light circulate: that is the deepest and most wonderful secret. The light is easy to move, but difficult to fix. If it is made to circulate long enough, then it crystallizes itself; that is the natural spirit-body. (p. 22)

This description perfectly matches the anatomical position and function of the pituitary gland. The SGF further affirms: "In the heavenly heart, life can be regulated... the heavenly heart is like the dwelling place, the light is the master." (p. 21) In physiology, we know the pituitary as the "master gland," regulating the entire endocrine system.

Thus, the light—the Golden Flower—is the Christ within, the true Master.

The Bible repeatedly uses the phrase "dwelling place" in this same sense. Psalm 90 opens, "Lord, thou hast been our dwelling place in all generations." In Psalm 91, a special promise is given: "He that dwelleth in the secret place of the most High shall abide under the shadow of the Almighty... Because thou hast made the Lord... thy habitation; There shall no evil befall thee... neither shall any plague come nigh thy dwelling." Psalm 23 ends triumphantly: "...and I shall dwell in the house of the Lord forever." Likewise, Psalm 27 declares: "One thing have I desired of the Lord... that I may dwell in the house of the Lord all the days of my life."

These passages affirm the importance of directing our consciousness toward the center of the forehead and all that it symbolizes: love, glory, unity, and Universal Consciousness.

In Revelation, the four beasts and twenty-four elders bow before the throne—mirroring the SGF's image of servants willingly obeying the master. Physiologically, this aligns with the pituitary's role in governing the body. However, its function may be overridden by demands from the lower centers, which is why the seventh church is described as "lukewarm."

The light is easy to move, but difficult to fix.

We often feel this movement of light during a stirring gospel song, a powerful sermon, or an inspiring film. We may vow to live differently, only to return the next day to our usual concerns. These temporary moments do move the light within—activating the endocrine system—but they rarely result in lasting change. For transformation to be enduring, the light must be fixed.

The SGF provides the method:

> Fixating contemplation is indispensable; it ensures making fast of the enlightenment... When the flight of the thoughts keeps extending further, one should stop and begin contemplating. Let one contemplate and then start fixating again. That is the double method of making fast the enlightenment. It means the circulation of the light. The circulation is fixation. The light is contemplation. Fixation without contemplation is circulation without light.

> Contemplation without fixation is light without circulation! Take note of that! (p. 36)

In meditation, the mantra circulates the light and stimulates the endocrine system. Silence allows the secretions to settle, re-patterning the body. This "double method" of activation and stillness enables true transformation. When thoughts wander, we return to the mantra to reignite the light. That light corresponds to the Pineal—the Christ center. Over time, this process reprograms the body's cellular response. Such transformation is necessary if we are to grow into the capacity to genuinely love our enemies, as Christ did when he said, "Father, forgive them, for they know not what they do."

○					
●	Pineal	Logos	Yang	Human Nature Li	Hsing
○					
○					
○					
●	Lyden	Eros	Yin	Life K'an	Ming
○					

Figure 20: Parallel Reference in the SFG to the Lyden/Pineal

What is the goal of meditation? Both the SGF and the Readings agree: to restore unity within the divided self. The SGF says:

> ...when the one note of individuation enters into the birth, human nature and life are divided in two. From this time on, if the utmost silence is not achieved, human nature and life never see each other again. (p. 23)

Figure 20 shows how "human nature" (*hsing*) corresponds to the Pineal, and "life" (*ming*) to the Lyden.

As stated in the SGF: "When the one note of individuation, the soul, enters into the birth, human nature and life are divided in two." **This mirrors what the Readings describe:** at the moment of conception, the first cell remains one—as we are one with God—but this oneness becomes functionally divided. Just as God, in His desire for companionship, divided Himself, so too is this cell divided in function. Its polarities manifest as the Lyden and the Pineal.

The SGF continues:

> Before the parents have begotten the child, the breath of life is complete, and the embryo is perfect. But when the embryo moves and the embryo vesicle is torn, it is as if a man lost his footing on a high mountain: with a cry the man plunges down to earth, and from then on human nature and life are divided. From this moment human nature can no longer see life nor life human nature. And now fate takes its course: youth passes over into maturity, maturity into old age, and old age into woe. (p. 70)

> If a dying man does not know this germinal vesicle, he will not find the unity of consciousness and life in a thousand births, nor in ten thousand aeons. (p. 70)

Here, the "embryo vesicle" and the "germinal vesicle" refer to the soul. This shared insight between the SGF and the Readings provides a major key. Few teachings offer such a direct explanation of the soul's entry into material existence. That the Lyden/Pineal connection is the seat of the soul—and that a division occurs even in the earliest stages of embryonic development—is remarkable. More astounding still is that this microcosmic separation reflects the macrocosmic event: God's division of Himself in the act of creation, motivated by the desire for companionship. As scripture affirms, *"God so loved the world..."*

In creating both Father and children, God initiated a polarity—positive and negative—that will only be healed when the children return to oneness with Him. The Readings say plainly: *"God is lonely without us."* (254-76)

Each time a child is conceived, this polarity is expressed in the physical body through which a soul incarnates. The separation remains until the soul remembers its divine origin. Only when it longs deeply for reunion—both with itself and with God—can healing begin. That restoration is possible only through the reuniting of the Lyden and Pineal in deep meditation.

At the moment of each physical conception, the soul's focal point of awareness rests in the lower self—centered in the

Lyden. This pattern of separation may persist across many lifetimes. Deep meditation is the singular means through which the Lyden and Pineal may be brought into unified function. This requires a conscious dedication to a high spiritual ideal. The Lyden is associated with life (*ming*), ordinary existence. When united with the Pineal, human nature (*hsing*), the soul awakens to enlightenment — Christ Consciousness, which is the awareness of Oneness.

The Readings describe this unity as *attunement* or *at-one-ment*. The SGF and the Book of Revelation both liken it to a marriage:

> The trigram K'an, water, the Abysmal, is the opposite of Li. It represents the region of eros, while Li stands for logos. Li is the sun, K'an the moon. The marriage of K'an and Li is the secret magical process which produces the child, the new man. The trigram Ken, mountain, Keeping Still, is the symbol of meditation, which, by keeping external things quiescent, gives life to the inner world. Therefore, Ken is the place where death and life meet.

These symbols reinforce the parallels between the Readings and the SGF. The "secret magical spell" that produces the child mirrors Revelation 12:2—*"a woman bearing a child."* Just as the Readings emphasize the interconnected roles of the Lyden, Pineal, and pituitary, so too does the SGF describe the energetic components of attunement:

> The way to the Elixir of Life knows as supreme magic, seed-water, spirit-fire, and thought-earth: these three. What is

> seed-water? It is the true one energy of former heaven (*eros*). Spirit-fire is the light (*logos*). Thought-earth is the heavenly heart of the middle dwelling (*intuition*). Spirit-fire is used for effecting, thought-earth for substance, and seed-water for the foundation. (p. 25)

We find a powerful parallel to this threefold structure in Reading 262-20:

> In the body we find that which connects the Pineal, the pituitary, the Lyden, may be truly called the silver cord, or the golden cup that may be filled with a closer walk with that which is the Creative Essence in physical, mental and spiritual life...

Pituitary	○	Thought - Earth
Pineal	○	Spirit - Fire
Thyroid	○	
Thymus	○	
Solar Plexus	○	
Lyden	○	Seed - Water
Gonads	○	

Figure 21: The Way to the Elixir of Life

In the Readings, meditation begins by awakening the spirit in the Lyden. This, in turn, activates the gonads—the power generators—symbolized in the SGF as *seed-water* (eros). That energy rises to the Pineal, the light, *spirit-fire*, or *logos*—the realm of the Mind. And as the Readings often state, *Mind is the builder*. Thus, when the SGF says "spirit-fire is used for effecting," it speaks to this same function of the mind as the creative agent.

When the Readings address the Trinity—Father, Son, and Holy Spirit—they reveal that in the Earth plane, the Father is represented by the body, the physical, the whole. Likewise, in the SGF, *thought-earth* is called the heavenly heart, intuition, and the base of substance.

The SGF offers detailed instructions for meditation:

> Only after concentrated work of a hundred contiguous days will the light be genuine; then only will it become spirit-fire. After a hundred days there develops by itself in the midst of the light a point of the true light-pole (yang). Then suddenly there develops the seed pearl. It is as if man and woman embraced and a conception took place. Then one must be quite still and wait. The circulation of the light is the epoch of fire. (p. 31)

The *true light-pole* here refers to the establishment of the Pineal's authority—the ascension of the Christ-conscious center over the instincts of the lower self, centered in the Lyden.

John the Baptist proclaimed that he baptized with water, but that Jesus would baptize with fire. In the trigrams of the *Secret of the Golden Flower* (SGF) text, K'an—the water center—corresponds to the Lyden gland, while Li—the sun and fire center—corresponds to the Pineal gland, symbolizing the Christ center.

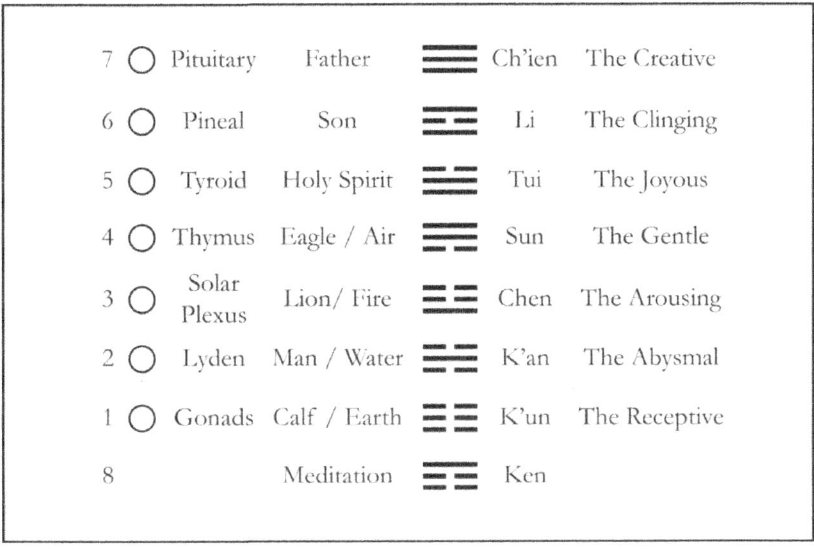

	Center		Trigram	
7	Pituitary	Father	Ch'ien	The Creative
6	Pineal	Son	Li	The Clinging
5	Tyroid	Holy Spirit	Tui	The Joyous
4	Thymus	Eagle / Air	Sun	The Gentle
3	Solar Plexus	Lion/ Fire	Chen	The Arousing
2	Lyden	Man / Water	K'an	The Abysmal
1	Gonads	Calf / Earth	K'un	The Receptive
8		Meditation	Ken	

Figure 22: The Centers and the SGF Trigrams

Both of these sacred sources—the Cayce Readings and the *SGF*—offer a parallel perspective in their sobering reflections on the nature of time. According to both texts, the journey Home may span eons upon eons. From the Readings: "Even though an entity in the earth's plane, in this life, may reach the years of fourscore and ten, these are as but moments in eternity." (640-1). And to several individuals, the Readings affirm: "Eternity is long with thy soul."

Similarly, the *SGF* states:

> In comparison with heaven and earth, man is like a mayfly. But compared to the great Way, heaven and earth, too, are like a bubble and a shadow." (p. 24)

> The life of man is like that of a mayfly: only the true human nature of the primal spirit can transcend the cycle of heaven and earth and the fate of the aeons. (p. 28)

Consider that some adult mayflies live only five minutes to a single day. The metaphor is staggering in its implications. Psalm 90, which contains allusions to reincarnation, expresses a similar longing: "How long, oh Lord, how long?"

The *SGF* takes meditation with the utmost seriousness:

> Children take heed! If for a day you do not practice meditation, this light streams out, who knows whither? If you only meditate for a quarter of an hour, by it you can do away with the ten thousand aeons and a thousand births. All methods end in quietness. This marvelous magic cannot be fathomed. p.33

> The circulation of the light is not only a circulation of the seed-blossom of the individual body, but it is even a circulation of the true, creative formative energies. It is not a momentary fantasy, but the exhaustion of the cycle (soul-migrations) of all the aeons. Therefore, the duration of a breath means a year according to human reckoning and a

> hundred years measured by the long night of the nine paths (of reincarnations) p. 32
>
> One must not be content with small demands but must rise to the thought that all living creatures have to be redeemed. p. 48

The Readings likewise affirm that the goal of meditation and focused intention is not simply personal healing, but self-transformation so that we may become instruments of healing for others.

Our intentions—conscious, focused, and directed—are the most vital force in our lives.

Stanford University physicist William Tiller conducted experiments that vividly demonstrated the power of intention. He developed a device toward which a group of meditators would direct a specific, agreed-upon intention. The device was then activated and the effects of the intention were measured.

For example, an intention was directed ("imprinted") in the device to raise the pH of a vessel of water one full pH unit, without the addition of any chemicals or change in the environment. A pH increase of one full pH unit was consistently and repeatedly achieved. Further, his experiments proved that the distance between the device and the vessel of water made no difference. One experiment raised the pH of a test vessel over 5,600 miles away with no physical link or connection. Tiller's results were repeatedly reproduced in other labs with the same results. This paved the way for other as

Tiller's books and White Papers document the positive effect of intention broadcasts to decrease human anxiety as well as marked benefit for children diagnosed with Autism Spectrum Disorder. His seminal body of work on intention is both rich and profound and his measurable and positive outcomes eventually led to subtle-energy broadcasting services to increase physical and mental health in human beings.

Thoughts are indeed "things"—especially those empowered by meditation. Such thoughts can exert real, measurable effects on physical objects, particularly on living organisms—and most especially on individuals in need. Years ago, polygraph expert Cleve Backster connected the electrodes of his lie detector to a rhododendron. Simply thinking about burning the plant triggered an immediate, measurable response. This story inspired a psychic to share an experience of seeing the auras of garden flowers, which extended toward some people and withdrew from others.

We are called to be healers. In our intentions, we must not be satisfied with minor aspirations. We are in this for the long journey. Yet we are promised a life more glorious than we can presently comprehend—through the work of Jesus and the ever-present Spirit of the Christ. As Scripture assures us:

"Eye hath not seen, nor ear heard, neither have entered into the heart of man, the things which God hath prepared for them that love him." (1 Cor. 2:9)

Much is said today about acting from the heart rather than the head—emphasizing emotions and intuition over pure intellect. The *SGF*, however, offers a more nuanced perspective on the heart. It differentiates between the heavenly heart—associated with the pituitary—and the physical heart as understood anatomically. The *SGF* observes:

> This lower fleshly heart has the shape of a large peach: it is covered by the wings of the lungs, supported by the liver, and served by the bowels. This heart is dependent on the outside world. If a man does not eat for one day, it feels extremely uncomfortable.
>
> The lower heart moves like a strong, powerful commander who despises the heavenly ruler because of his weakness and has usurped leadership in affairs of state... When rule in the centre is thus in order, all those rebellious heroes will present themselves with lances reversed, ready to take orders. (p. 25)

This warning regarding the "fleshly heart" applies not only to the heart/thymus center but to all four lower centers. Therefore, when we speak of acting from the heart, let us invoke the heavenly heart—the divine center—not the emotionally reactive, fleshly heart. The weakness of the heavenly ruler is reminiscent of the lukewarm nature of the Church of Laodicea—associated with the pituitary center. Ideally, the energies of the lower heart may be harnessed to awaken the power of the higher, heavenly heart.

In the continuation of this section, the *SGF* describes a pivotal moment in meditation:

> Then with both eyes one illumines the house of the Abysmal [water, K'an]. Related things attract each other. Thus, the polarized light-line of the Abysmal presses upward. It is not only the light in the abyss, but it is creative light which meets creative light. As soon as these two substances meet each other, they unite inseparably, and there develops an unceasing life... (p. 55)

When the Abysmal (K'an) and the Clinging (Li) unite, the Golden Flower emerges. The text explains:

> The golden color is white, and therefore white snow is used as a symbol. (p. 62)

We are again reminded with urgency:

> "Children take heed!"

Chapter 11
Religions and Archetypes

WE HAVE DEVELOPED an understanding of archetypes as universal patterns inherent in every soul. A work becomes a classic when it resonates with these patterns, possessing a universal appeal that touches many people. Not every creation with archetypal elements fully embodies the complete archetype; however, the more faithfully a work aligns with archetypal structure, the greater its potential to become a classic. Archetypal patterns can be found in art, music, literature, and all religious traditions. In every case, works that contain archetypal elements have the potential to instruct and illuminate. A few examples will help illustrate this principle.

Hinduism

In Hinduism, as in Christianity, there exists a triune conception of divinity. Corresponding to the Christian Father, Son, and Holy Spirit are Brahma, Vishnu, and Shiva. Brahma is the Creator; Vishnu, sometimes incarnated as Krishna, is the Preserver; and Shiva, often called the Destroyer, represents the

Spirit—the single, unifying force. Shiva is the symbol of pure energy, and as such, is said to manifest in countless forms. He embodies both creation and destruction, the source and sustainer of the universe. Often portrayed as the Lord of the Dance in statuary, Shiva symbolizes everything: motion and stillness, male and female, light and darkness, ascetic and sensual lover—all opposites reconciled.

In Joseph Dye's *Ways to Shiva*, from which I draw extensively, he writes:

> Shiva is called in sacred texts by countless names. Some, such as the Three-Eyed One and the Blue-Throated One, describe his forms or attributes; others, such as the Destroyer of the Three Cities and the Lord of the Dance, refer to his mythical activities. (pp. 45–46)

The "Three Cities" may symbolize the three higher spiritual centers, suggesting that Shiva can also destroy their spiritual functions.

One Cayce Reading also touches on this Hindu trinity. For a metaphysics teacher with past lives in Asia, the Reading says:

> . . . the Father, the Son and the Holy Spirit are one. God as the Father, Creator, Maker; the Son as the Way, the Mind, the Activity, the Preserver; the Holy Spirit as the motivative force—or as the destroyer or the maker alive, dependent upon the manners in which these influences are used by the individual entity … (2429-1)

Notably, in this case—speaking to someone versed in comparative religion—the Cayce Source employs the Hindu-like terms "Preserver" and "Destroyer."

In our study of Revelation, Chapter 9 speaks of an angel with the key to the bottomless pit, named Abaddon or Apollyon—both meaning "destroyer." This relates to the fifth angel and the fifth spiritual center: the thyroid gland, which in the trinity corresponds to the Spirit. Deuteronomy 30:19 declares, "I have set before you life and death, blessing and cursing: therefore choose life…" The thyroid, which governs metabolism, has both anabolic and catabolic functions—it builds up and breaks down—making it symbolic of both Spirit and destruction.

According to the Readings, the fifth center is blue and located at the throat. Remember, Dye describes Shiva as the Three-Eyed One and the Blue-Throated One. The parallels are remarkable.

Dye's book also includes an image of Shiva with a blazing lingam behind him, while Brahma and Vishnu bow before him. The caption reads:

> According to legend, Shiva appeared as a fiery lingam pillar when Vishnu and Brahma each claimed to have created the universe. Vishnu, in his boar form, dove deep to find the lingam's base; Brahma, in goose form, flew upward to find its top. When both failed, Shiva revealed himself as the true Creator of the universe.

Recall what the Readings say about First Cause: God's desire for companionship with Himself produced separation—the "reverse of love." Thus, as God divided Himself into Father and souls, those souls inherited an inner inclination toward separation and, ultimately, rebellion.

This mirrors Shiva's rebellion against Brahma and Vishnu. The complexity of Shiva aligns with Abaddon—the destroyer of the fifth angel in Revelation, the angel of the bottomless pit. The fifth center represents choice, desire, will, and self-will—all facets of Spirit, the third person of the trinity. It is therefore also the origin of the spirit of rebellion. Even in his destructive aspects, Shiva remains a Divine figure—a God.

7th	Father	Brahma
6th	Son	Vishnu
5th	Holy Spirit	Shiva - Destroyer

Figure 23: The Trinities

In Reading 281-51, which discusses the concepts of love and the reverse of love, we also find insight into the contradictory nature of the mind. The mind can both conceive of God and devise means for the destruction of others—unaware that such destruction ultimately harms the self.

Understanding the Anti-Christ

This offers context for the religious fervor that can be stirred by the spirit of the anti-Christ. It also sheds light on the emotional intensity surrounding firearms and mass shootings. These acts often stem not from simple madness but from a perverse form of religious zeal. Surprisingly, individuals driven by such fervor may consider themselves devout Christians—yet their behavior aligns more closely with followers of Shiva than of Vishnu, and certainly not of Jesus.

Jungian psychology, which resonates with the Cayce Readings, teaches that everyone has a shadow side. The more that darkness is denied, the more likely it will manifest destructively—in hatred and fear.

The only biblical references to "antichrist" appear in 1 John 2:18–22, which states:

> ... as you have heard that antichrist shall come, even now there are many antichrists; whereby we know that it is the last time.

The Bible, then, does not speak of *the* Antichrist, but of many antichrists. A Cayce Reading addresses this:

> Q-4: In what form does the anti-Christ come, spoken of in the Revelation?
>
> A-4: "In the spirit opposed to the spirit of truth. The fruits of the spirit of the Christ are love, joy, obedience, long-suffering, brotherly love, kindness. Against such there is no law. The spirit of hate, the anti-Christ, is contention, strife, fault-finding, lovers of self, lovers of praise. Those are the antichrist, and take possession of groups, masses, and show themselves even in the lives of men." (281-16)

We may expect such appearances even in modern times!

How does the spirit of hate take possession of the masses? It becomes a form of religion—the "spiritual negative." This corresponds to Shiva's dark side and to the Readings' concept of the "reverse of love." According to Jungians, the rise of the anti-Christ is both imminent and inevitable.

How can one individual expressing anti-Christ qualities "take possession of groups and masses"? A Cayce Reading offers this insight regarding the pituitary:

> To be purely material-minded… one fed upon spiritual things becomes a light that may shine from and in the darkest corner. One fed upon the purely material will become a Frankenstein… without a concept of any influence other than material or mental. (262-20)

Such a person becomes a Frankenstein—not as a monster, but as a *maker* of monsters.

In *On Being a Real Person* (1943), renowned preacher Harry Emerson Fosdick describes such individuals as "integrated." He includes figures like Hitler and Napoleon, noting that such people do not need to be moral. "Men like Hitler… become the idol of millions, although they set the world destructively ablaze." (p. 39)

All cult-like behavior has an addictive component. It shifts political discourse from the rational to the emotional.

The Reading above refers to singleness of purpose. When a person of great ability focuses solely on personal power or ambition, they may become a Frankenstein—or an anti-Christ. Frankenstein, remember, was the *creator* of monsters.

We see this dynamic in modern culture. The danger lies in underestimating the power of evil, or not recognizing it, as it manifests today.

Mass movements are rarely built on shared ideals of the common good, because consensus is difficult. Instead, they are formed around a common enemy—Hitler did this with the Jews. Hate unifies, and its contagion can spread rapidly. In democratic societies, this strategy can even influence elections. When masses begin to hate, even "good" people may come to hate the haters in turn. Many still hate Hitler today.

Yet hate harms the hater. One of Jesus' hardest commands is to "love your enemies." As he said in Matthew 5:44:

"Love your enemies, bless them that curse you, do good to them that hate you, and pray for them which despitefully use you, and persecute you."

This is not merely moral advice—it is vital for spiritual growth. Hate blocks the flow of the Spirit through the third center.

It is also striking that both the Bible and the Cayce Readings affirm that no one holds power except by divine permission. The Readings state:

> For none are in power but have been given the opportunity by the will of the Father. (3976-18)

Similarly, in John 19:11, Jesus tells Pilate:

> Thou couldest have no power at all against me, except it were given thee from above.

This does not imply that God prefers evil rulers. Rather, through the law of karma, the consciousness of a people determines the leader they receive.

More on Hinduism

In temples devoted to Shiva, the bull Nandi always gazes into the sanctuary's center, where a lingam resides. In Revelation, the first church—associated with the gonads—is symbolized by a calf, which in Shaivism corresponds to Nandi. The gonads are not just sexual glands; they are the generative power behind all spiritual activity. In Shaivite worship, the first and fifth centers are thus closely linked.

The first center provides generative power; the fifth, representing the Holy Spirit, is also a source of power. Together, these allow Shiva to be viewed as the "Creator of the Universe." This linkage is mirrored in the Nandi/lingam symbolism.

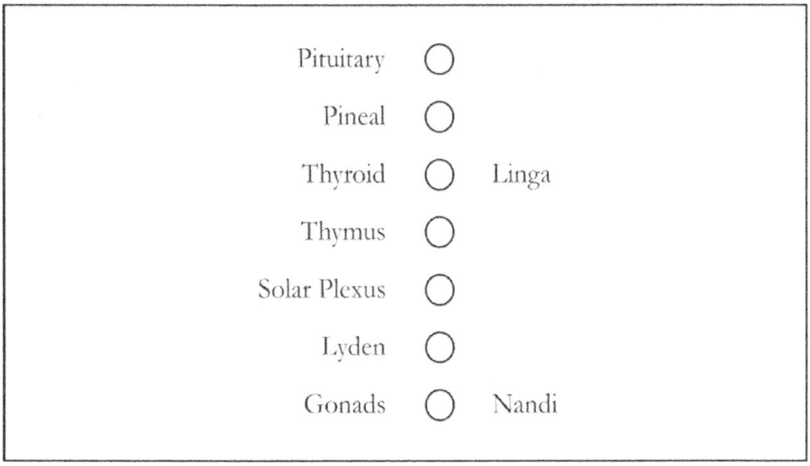

Pituitary	○	
Pineal	○	
Thyroid	○	Linga
Thymus	○	
Solar Plexus	○	
Lyden	○	
Gonads	○	Nandi

Figure 24: Dynamics of the Main Centers Empowering Shiva Worship

Just as Shaivism can be analyzed through dominant energy centers, so too can other religions be understood by the centers they activate. Different musical styles, rituals, chants, incenses, prayers, and meditation techniques stimulate the endocrine system in unique ways, resulting in varied spiritual experiences.

This same arousal of energies appears in ancient war cries and even in the frenzied cheers of modern sports and political rallies—a positive force, yet directed toward unrighteous ends.

Archetypes and Biochemistry

As previously discussed, there exists a biochemistry of consciousness—and thus a biochemistry underlying religious and spiritual experiences. These distinct chemical processes could be considered *elixirs* of awareness. When a seasoned practitioner trains a novice in a specific form of worship, and the novice has a similar, valid spiritual experience, it is natural for both to believe they have found the true path.

For instance, in certain charismatic and Pentecostal traditions, speaking in tongues is often seen as definitive proof of baptism by the Holy Spirit. In such experiences, the rising spiritual energy activates the thyroid—the fifth center—and in turn stimulates the vocal cords. Faith, closely associated with this center, becomes the gateway to such ecstatic states. Some adherents even go so far as to handle snakes, as suggested in certain Biblical passages, believing their "faith" will protect them from harm. Such encounters with serpent-power—or kundalini energy—are rarely successful.

In Islam, which has a historically militaristic origin, the emphasis tends to be on the solar plexus center. This energy configuration lends itself to a combative disposition. Daoism, on the other hand, emphasizes the gentle, flowing nature of water, resonating with the second center. In Christianity, a particular subset—such as certain Catholic traditions—focuses on the image of the "bleeding-heart" Jesus, highlighting the heart or fourth center. Some forms of Buddhist meditation are deeply contemplative, activating the Pineal gland and engaging higher mental faculties.

Catholicism often emphasizes the One True Church, represented symbolically by the pituitary gland and a sense of universal consciousness. Yet, paradoxically, it remains preoccupied with issues surrounding sexuality—stemming from the first and second centers. This is reflected in official

Church doctrines opposing birth control and abortion, as well as in the call for celibate priesthoods, which have too often been plagued by sexual scandal.

Cultural anthropologist Ruth Benedict, in her study *The Chrysanthemum and the Sword*, explores the Japanese psyche through the dual symbolism of beauty and violence. The chrysanthemum represents the thymus (Venus), and the sword corresponds to the solar plexus (Mars). The Japanese emphasis on "Hara," or spiritual and emotional strength centered in the belly, reinforces this archetypal pattern.

These examples illustrate how specific religious experiences correspond to the activation of different endocrine centers. Because practitioners in these traditions share similar physiological and spiritual experiences, they often find these practices deeply authentic and validating.

The Tibetan Dorje

One of the central symbols in Tibetan Buddhism is the Dorje, also known as the Vajra or Diamond Sceptre. We have previously discussed the Lyden/Pineal connection as an extended cellular structure of profound importance—serving as the seat of the soul. The Dorje is an archetypal image that visually parallels this concept.

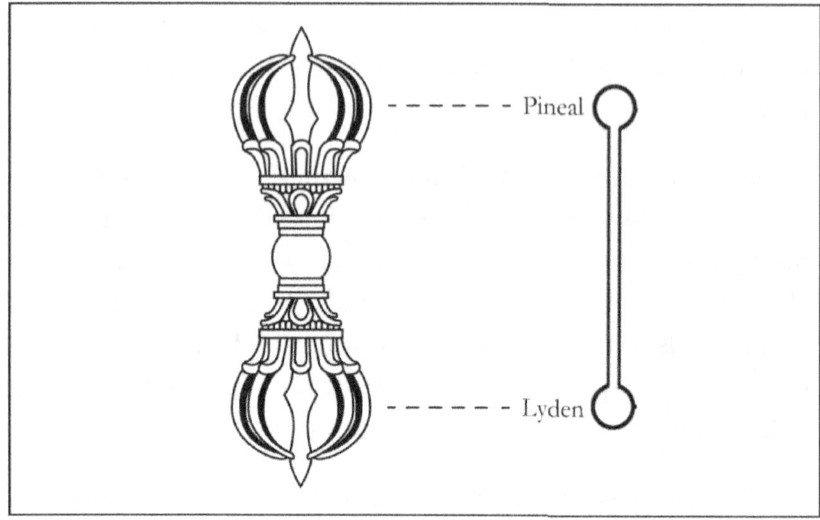

Figure 25: The Dorje

In *Foundations of Tibetan Buddhism*, Lama Govinda offers a vivid description of the Vajra:

> The mind alone is the radiant jewel, from which all things borrow their temporal reality. He who possesses this shining jewel overcomes death and rebirth and gains immortality and liberation. But this jewel cannot be found anywhere except in the lotus (padma) of one's own heart. In later forms of Buddhism, the idea of the jewel took the form of the Diamond Sceptre, the Vajra, and became as such the most important symbol for the transcendental qualities of Buddhism. The Vajra is regarded as the symbol of highest spiritual power—irresistible and invincible. As a visible symbol, the Vajra takes the form of a sceptre—the emblem of supreme, sovereign power—and therefore it is correct to

> call it a 'diamond sceptre.' Its center is a sphere representing the undifferentiated seed or germ of the universe—the 'bindu' (dot, zero, drop, smallest unit). Potential force is often shown as a spiral emerging from this center. From the unity at the center arise two opposite poles, unfolding as lotus blossoms, symbolizing the polarity of all conscious existence. The vajra … expresses both polarity and the relative dualism of consciousness and the world, while also postulating the unity of opposites…. He who discovers the Philosopher's Stone—the radiant jewel (mani) of the enlightened mind within his own heart—transforms mortal awareness into immortal consciousness, perceives the infinite in the finite, and turns Samsara into Nirvana. (*FTM*, pp. 61, 65)

In its physical form, the Vajra serves as a healing instrument. In its symbolic form, it becomes a profound focus for meditation. Its structure precisely affirms the universality and central role of the Lyden/Pineal interaction as the soul's dwelling and the pathway to enlightenment. The Vajra represents the dynamics of this interaction and mirrors the symbolism found in *The Secret of the Golden Flower*, where the relationship between life and human nature is mapped through spiritual centers. Its emphasis on the mind directly parallels the link between the mind, the Pineal gland, and the Christ—the Logos, the builder of the soul.

The Wizard of Oz and Temptation

Fairy tales can also express deep archetypal truths, sometimes unconsciously. *The Wizard of Oz* is a modern archetypal classic. Let's examine it through this lens: Uncle Henry, Dorothy, and Aunt Em may be interpreted as symbolic of the Father, the Son, and the Spirit, respectively. Dorothy's trouble begins with her dog, Toto—an aspect of herself that causes mischief. Even before the storm, Toto is a source of disruption. When the storm arrives, Dorothy chases after Toto and is swept into the world of Oz.

In Oz, as in the Revelation's vision of four beasts, we encounter four traveling companions:8

- Gonads – the calf – Earth – Scarecrow
- Lyden – man – Water – Dorothy
- Solar Plexus – lion – Fire – the Cowardly Lion
- Thymus – tin-man – Air – the Heart center

The Emerald City represents the fourth center, the heart, traditionally associated with the color green. Dorothy, like many spiritual seekers, initially believes that the heart center—the city of Oz—holds something miraculous. Yet, when she arrives, she finds only illusion. The "wizard" is humbug. The *Secret of the Golden Flower* reminds us that it is not the fleshly heart (thymus) we seek, but the "Heavenly Heart"—the pituitary.

In our daily lives, we often mistake this present world—the "Oz" of our senses—for reality. We see it in vivid technicolor, while our spiritual Home seems dull and monochrome, like Kansas. Yet it is the true Home. Our longing to remain in this sensory "Oz" consciousness keeps us returning to the earth plane. Though we search here, our salvation is not found in the illusions of this realm.

The *Wizard of Oz* clearly follows the Prodigal Son archetype: Dorothy leaves home, finds herself in a strange land, and longs to return. The yellow brick road symbolizes the Lyden/Pineal pathway—the Appian Way. The good and wicked witches reflect the spiritual forces around us, working for either good or evil. Her ultimate return, by clicking the red slippers three times, symbolizes a transformative understanding of spiritual law.

Figure 25: The Relationship Between Oz and the Seven Centers

I noted earlier that Toto played a central role in Dorothy's journey into Oz. Let us explore this further. When we designate the roles of the seven spiritual centers, we find “man” present in both the upper three and the lower four centers. In the higher triad: Father, Son, Spirit, and Man. In the Revelation, the four beasts of the lower centers are: a calf, a man, a lion, and an eagle.

In Oz, Dorothy corresponds to the “man” of the four beasts. If we see her as representing the Son while still in Kansas, she embodies both poles of the Lyden/Pineal axis. Since these centers are truly one cell, it is fitting that Dorothy represents both. In the Lord’s Prayer, the second center corresponds to “lead us not into temptation.” The Lyden, as the seat of the soul, is the part of consciousness that can become lost—symbolized by Dorothy’s journey into Oz.

Toto, who leads her into trouble, represents the temptation inherent in that center. We can expand this symbolism with other examples.

The Qur’an tells of sleepers in a cave for 306 years. It mentions: some say there were five and their dog was the sixth; others say six and the dog was the seventh; still others say seven and the dog was the eighth. Allah alone knows the truth.

How many spiritual centers are there? Tibetan systems sometimes combine the first and second, and the sixth and seventh, into unified pairs. This makes sense: the Lyden is located in the gonads (first center), and Jesus says he does only what he sees the Father doing (sixth center as the open door).

This consolidation may explain the Tibetan system of the five dhyani-Buddhas.

The sleepers-in-the-cave metaphor suggests that we may remain dormant for eons, never awakening our centers to true spiritual life. The Cayce Readings affirm that when incarnate, the soul slumbers and dreams. But why is there always a dog with the sleepers?

In Goethe's *Faust*, a disillusioned Faust ventures out on Easter morning to observe celebrants. Upon returning, a black poodle follows him home. In his study, the dog transforms into Mephistopheles. The devil offers Faust the fulfillment of all his desires. Faust accepts—and thus succumbs to temptation.

These symbolic dogs resemble Toto. They also parallel the mysterious passage in Revelation 17, which speaks of a beast that "was, and is not," yet is the eighth:

> The beast that thou sawest was, and is not… and the beast that was, and is not, even he is the eighth, and is of the seven, and goeth into perdition. (Rev. 17:7,11)

This "eighth" beast, which carries the woman—Mystery Babylon—symbolizes the lower self from which we must be liberated. The lower self, like the woman, is carried by a beast that is always present, yet illusory. This is temptation.

The dog with the cave sleepers is a metaphor for the soul's temptation to slumber endlessly. As the Readings say, in the earth plane the soul slumbers and dreams—just like Snow White.

The Lyden's temptation is to project energy outward rather than raise it inward. The *Secret of the Golden Flower* cautions:

> Children, take heed! If for a day you do not practice meditation, this light streams out—who knows whither? If you only meditate for a quarter of an hour, by it you can do away with ten thousand aeons and a thousand births.

CHAPTER 12
DESTINY

WHAT THEN, IN the vastness of infinity and eternity, is to become of us? What lies ahead, and what is our task? The Readings affirm that preparation for the soul's evolution has spanned thousands—even millions—of years, and it will continue for thousands more. Through the coming of the Christ in Jesus, we are given the potential for significant advancement. Yet much remains to be done.

The period just before Jesus' appearance was described as the darkest in human history. Against this backdrop came a new promise: we now have a Savior, an Advocate, and an archetypal Pattern that assures us of real progress in the development of our souls. Still, as emphasized throughout this work, we must envision our journey in terms of eons—not merely the span of a single lifetime.

In a shorter timeframe, the Readings describe an era in which, for a thousand years, only attuned souls will be allowed to incarnate. This remarkable opportunity is designed to create a world more conducive to soul advancement, especially for those in distress. As the Readings urge, "Be ye all determined to be in that number!"

Once we graduate from this solar system, we may move on to a more enlightened state of consciousness—perhaps aligned with the realms of Arcturus, which has been described as the consciousness center of our galaxy. Soul entanglement, Cayce said, exists throughout the universe, and some of us may choose to explore other systems. The Readings specifically mention the Pleiades, Orion, and Arcturus as such destinations.

As we contemplate the destiny of humanity—of God's children—the biblical notion of predestination comes into focus. Romans 8:29 tells us, "...whom He foreknew He also did predestinate to be conformed to the image of His Son, that he might be the firstborn among many brethren." All souls were created in His image.

Whom did He foreknow? Ephesians 1:4–5 explains: "According as he hath chosen us in him before the foundation of the world." We were created in His image, chosen before the world began. The ultimate destiny of every soul is union with God.

Scripture tells us that God is not willing that any soul should perish—and the Readings affirm that nothing truer has ever been said. God is love and forgiveness. Only the unloving, unforgiving believer could imagine that God preordained some souls for heaven and others for hell. Such a view casts a profoundly negative light on the God who *is* Love. The destiny of every soul is to return to unity with God and to the love of our Father.

Why, then, does it take us so long, especially when we are free to return at any moment? The issue lies in our misunderstanding of time.

To God, a thousand years is like a single day. The real question is: how long will we continue to resist God's love? When He says, "I stand at the door and knock," it signals an ongoing, gentle invitation for transformation and acceptance of His presence. The Christ spirit is always with us—ever knocking at the door of our hearts.

The Way of Love is the way of service. We have discussed the purpose of Jesus' resurrected, glorified body. The true meaning of "glory" is the capacity to serve.

In the second volume of *A Search for God*, three lessons explore Destiny: Destiny of the Mind, Destiny of the Body, and Destiny of the Soul. The mind and soul are destined to return to God. We are assured that we will, at some future point, become one with the Divine. But what of the body? There is a physical body we develop over time, and a flesh body which we discard at death.

We are given the opportunity to develop a perfect body — "unto a perfect man," as the Bible puts it. According to the Readings, this glorified body is a gift we can return to God. It signifies the soul's readiness to serve more completely in love for God's lost children. We see this ideal fulfilled in Jesus' ministry to His friends after the resurrection.

In Daoism, as presented in *The Secret of the Golden Flower*, there is the promise of becoming one of the immortals. In a surprising affirmation, the Readings even suggest that some individuals have never experienced death. This concept, often the theme of science fiction—people who cannot die—echoes a deeper consciousness that immortals may indeed exist.

Each of us will ultimately determine the destiny of our own body. Will we aspire to build a glorified body, driven by an ideal of ever-deepening service?

The Readings also emphasize that true happiness is never found in selfish pursuits but only through serving others—through aiding another soul. Happiness flows from allowing God's love and power to pass through us in support of someone else. When a seeker once asked whether she was dedicating enough time to soul development, the Source replied, "soul development should be given precedence over all other endeavors." The steps to soul development are clear, and may be summed up in three words: Aspire, Attune, and Apply.

Aspiration: Our spiritual ideal is our guiding aspiration. It must represent a wholehearted dedication to a life of loving service. The Readings stress that the most important experience for any soul is to know its spiritual ideal. *The key is to compel, induce, and train the mind to dwell upon that ideal.* Mind is the builder, and we are co-creators with God. Every thought shapes what we are becoming. Thoughts are real—they become either crimes or miracles.

Attunement: Attunement is best achieved through regular meditation. We must bring our bodies and minds into alignment with our spiritual ideal. The high spiritual quality of the soul can only be fully expressed through the body when Oneness is manifest—especially through activation of the Lyden/Pineal center in harmony with the ideal. This is essential for attaining higher consciousness. It demands deep meditation. Remember: all we can know of God must flow through us.

Application: We are urged to *do* what we already know to do. Only then can the next step be revealed. When facing a health challenge, for example, we may search broadly for treatment. But we already know that drinking six to eight glasses of water daily, eating life-filled foods, and engaging in physical activity to circulate the blood—all these are essential supports to healing. If we neglect what we know, how can we expect to be shown more? To know and not do is to create inner conflict—something utterly incompatible with the quest for Oneness. This is a serious spiritual problem.

Application also involves how we treat others. We are all god-beings. The way we treat others is, in essence, the way we treat Christ, since the "Christ in you" is present in every soul. American author James Truslow Adams admonished, "There is so much good in the worst of us, and so much bad in the best of us, there can hardly be room for any of us to talk poorly about the rest of us." The Readings remind us that in the material world, only the "little things" truly matter.

Soul development depends upon these steps. There are no shortcuts. We must all become seekers. We each have much to learn—and much to unlearn. Often, it is easier to accept a new truth than to let go of an old belief. Yet growth demands change. And we must remember: "Eye has not seen, nor ear heard" the wonders awaiting us in higher dimensions of consciousness.

Jesus tells us that He came to reveal the truth—and that the truth will set us free. He came so that our joy may be complete. We may fulfill our destiny when our ideal is rooted in service, and we may discover the fullness of joy only through a soul-purpose—a life devoted to service.

The *Secret of the Golden Flower* affirms: "The maxim handed down to us is to take in hand the work on human nature." (p. 21) This "work on human nature" is precisely the work of soul development.

Scripture affirms the necessity of two witnesses. The Readings and *The Secret of the Golden Flower* stand as such witnesses—each illuminating the challenges and glories of the soul's journey. Through these guides, we are offered a path to service, enlightenment, and immortality. And we are reminded:

You are gods, children of the Most High, all of you!

WORKS CITED

Aurobindo, Sri. *Essays on the Gita*. Sri Aurobindo Library. New York, 1950.

Bach, Marcus. *The Inner Ecstasy*. York, 1975.

Benson, Herbert. *The Relaxation Response*. William Morrow, New York. 1975.

Bock, Steven J. *Stay Young the Melatonin Way*. Dutton. New York, NY.

Boring, Edwin. *A History of Experimental Psychology, 2nd Ed,* Appleton-Century-Crofts, NY, 1950.

Boyles, C. Allan. *The Way*. Theophysics Publishing. Columbia, MD. 1990. Also: *God and Quantum Physics, Wheatmark*, Tucson, AZ

Browning, Robert. *The Complete Poetical Works of Browning*. Houghton Mifflin. Boston. 1895.

Bucke, Richard. *Cosmic Consciousness*. E.P. Dutton. New York. 1969.

Cayce, Edgar. *A Search for God*. A.R.E. Press. 1942.

Cayce, Edgar. *Edgar Cayce and The Secret of the Golden Flower*. A.R.E. Press. Virginia Beach, Va. 2020.

Cayce, Edgar. *Meditation Part I: Healing, Prayer and The Revelation.* A.R.E. Press. 1974.

Conant, James. *On Understanding Science.* Yale University Press. 1947.

Danforth, William. *I Dare You.* American Youth Foundation. St. Louis Mo. 1972

DeChardin, Teilhard. *The Heart of Matter.* Harcourt, Brace, Jovanovich. New York.

Dye, Joseph. *Ways to Shiva: Life and Ritual in Hindu India.* Philadelphia Museum of Art. Philadelphia, Pa. 1980.

Edinger, Edward. *Archetype of the Apocalypse: A Jungian Study of the* Book of Revelation. Open Court, Ill. 1999.

Goethe, Johann. *Faust: A Tragedy.* The Modern Library. New York.

Govinda, Lama. *Foundations of Tibetan Mysticism.* Samuel Weiser. New York. 1956.

Greaves, Helen. *Testimony of Light.* Neville Spearman. Suffolk. 1969.

Hall, Manley. *Reincarnation: Cycle of Necessity.* The Philosophical Research Society. Los Angeles, Ca. 1939.

Hudson, Thomas. *The Law of Psychic Phenomena.* Samuel Weiser. New York. 1968.

Jung, Carl. *The Undiscovered Self.* Princeton University Press. 1957.

Kirkpatrick, Sidney. *Edgar Cayce: An American Prophet.* Penguin Putnam. New York. 2000.

Leininger, Bruce and Andrea. *Soul Survivor.* Grand Central Publishing. New York. 2009.

Michaelson, Jay. *God is Everything: The Radical Path of Nondual Judaism.* Shambala Publications. Boston, Ma. 2009.

Mohammed. *The Koran Interpreted.* Simon and Shuster. New York. 1955.

Monroe, Robert A. *Ultimate Journey.* Harmony Books. New York. 1994.

Montgomery, Ruth. *A Search for the Truth.*

Murphy, Gardner. *The Challenge of Psychical Research: A Primer of Psychical Research.* Harper and Brothers. New York. 1961.

Pogano, John. *Healing Psoriasis.* Wiley and Sons. Hoboken, NJ. 2009.

Polgar, Franz. *The Story of a Hypnotist.* Hermitage House. New York. 1951.

Puryear, Herbert and Thurston, Mark. *Meditation and the Mind of Man.* A.R.E. Press. Virginia Beach, Va. 1975.

Puryear, Herbert. *Why Jesus Taught Reincarnation.* New Paradigm Press. Scottsdale, Az. 1992. *The Edgar Cayce Primer*. Bantam Books. New York. 1982.

Rhine, J.B. *The Reach of the Mind.* William Sloan. New York. 1947.

Ritchie, George. *Return from Tomorrow*. Guideposts, Chosen Books. Carmel, NY. 1978.

Sheldrake, Rupert. *Dogs What Know When Their Owners Are Coming Home*. Three Rivers Press. New York. 1999.

Spinoza, Baruch. *The Philosophy of Spinoza.* Carlton House. New York.

Sugrue, Thomas. *There is a River.* Henry Holt. New York. 1942.

Tiller, William A. *Science and Human Transformation*. Pavior Publishing. Walnut Creek, CA. 1997. White Papers XVI, XXIV, XXX. www.tillerfoundation.org.

Van Auken, John. *Edgar Cayce on the Revelation: A Study Guide for Spiritualizing Body and Mind.* A.R.E. Press. Virginia Beach, Va. 2000.

Van Auken, John *Spiritual Breakthrough.* A.R.E. Press. Virginia Beach, Va. 1992. *Living in the Light.* A.R.E. Press. Virginia Beach, Va. 2025.

Watts, Alan. *The Book: On the Taboo Against Knowing Who You Are.* Vintage Books, Random House. New York. 1969.

Watts, Alan. *Beyond Theology: The Art of Godmanship.* Vintage Books, Random House. New York. 1964.

Wilhelm, Richard and Jung, Carl. *The Secret of the Golden Flower: A Chinese Book of Life.* Harcourt, Brace Jovanovich. San Francisco. 1962.

Readers may also wish to refer to the John Van Auken books, *Spiritual Breakthrough* and *Passage in Consciousness* for a deeper study of the soul's activity and processes in the altered states of consciousness afforded by deep meditation.

Other books by Herbert Puryear

Dreams: The Light of the Night

Day by Day

Meditation and the Mind of Man

Reflections on the Path

Sex and The Spiritual Path

The Cycles of Life

The Edgar Cayce Primer

Why Jesus Taught Reincarnation

About The Author

Herb Puryear has been a student of the Edgar Cayce Readings since he read *There Is a River* in 1951.

In 1957 after graduating from Stanford, he attended the University of North Carolina. His master's thesis and his doctoral dissertation were on dreams and dreaming. In 1962 Herb joined the psychology faculty at Trinity University in San Antonio. He received training from Milton Erikson and he is a certified hypnotherapist in the Eriksonian techniques. He also had a private practice in psychotherapy featuring dream interpretation, and he was a clinical consultant to the psychology department at the San Antonio State Hospital.

In 1969, he joined the A.R.E. in Virginia Beach where he worked both as Director of Education and Director of Research over his fourteen years on the staff.

Herb and his wife Anne incorporated The Logos Center in 1982. Along with developing the Center, Herb conducted Anne's psychic readings for more than twenty years.

About The Author

Made in United States
North Haven, CT
29 April 2026

10517946R00147